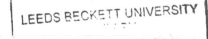
The Eternal Now

The Eternal Now

Paul Tillich

scm press

© Paul Tillich 1963
Preface © David H. Kelsey 2002

A catalogue record for this book is available
from the British Library

ISBN 0 334 02875 2

First published in 1963 by SCM Press
This new edition published in 2002
9–17 St Albans Place, London N1 0NX

www.scm-canterburypress.co.uk

SCM Press is a division of
SCM-Canterbury Press Ltd

Typeset by Rowland Phototypesetting Ltd,
Bury St Edmunds, Suffolk
Printed by Nørhaven Paperback A/S, Viborg, Denmark

Contents

To the memory of
HERMANN SCHAFFT
friend for more than
half a century

Preface

Paul Tillich (1886–1965) was one of the two most celebrated Christian theologians in the United States from the late 1940s to the late 1960s (the other was Reinhold Niebuhr, his colleague on the faculty of Union Theological Seminary in New York). During that time, Tillich preached the sermons and meditations collected here in American college and university chapels. Indeed, the publication of three collections of his sermons, of which this is the third (the other two are *Shaking the Foundations*, New York: Scribners, 1948, and *The New Being*, New York: Scribners, 1955), played a large role in his becoming a major 'public theologian' in America in the middle of the twentieth century. It was, in effect, the beginning for Tillich of prominence in a second career in an alien culture, using an unfamiliar language.

In Germany Tillich had already become a nationally recognized religious thinker by 1933, when the Nazi party suspended him from his faculty position in the Philosophy Department of the University of Frankfurt because of his published attack on Nazi ideology. As a young Lutheran pastor, four years after he had earned his doctorate in philosophical theology from the University of Breslau, Tillich had been drafted into the German army as a chaplain, serving with troops in the midst of the worst horrors of front-line fighting. The experience transformed him. Tillich's war experiences persuaded him that the core religious issue in the modern age is raised not, as it had been in past eras, by death or guilt but by all that threatens to make life meaningless. He saw himself as a Christian 'on the boundary' between religious and secular orientations, between divided classes and cultures, between faith and doubt. From the first lecture he gave after the war, in his first academic appointment at the University of Berlin, to his appointment at Frankfurt, the central focus of his theological work was the 'theology of culture'. And then, abruptly, this middle-aged academic had to flee Germany with his family for the United States, with its unfamiliar culture and a foreign language, where he was unknown.

Friends arranged a faculty appointment for him at Union Theological Seminary in New York City. For fifteen years Tillich taught at Union in relative obscurity. He learned to read and understand English quickly enough, but his heavy accent made it difficult for American students to understand him. Nor was it any easier for professional colleagues. The American intellectual world, especially among philosophers, was so different from Germany's that there was only a very small group of academics who had the frame of reference needed to grasp what he was up to theologically. Then suddenly, in the late 1940s, his published sermons, of all things, not his philosophical theology, became best-sellers. The media discovered him, his portrait appeared on the cover of *Time* magazine and Tillich became the most celebrated defender in two centuries of American Christianity against its cultured despisers.

Perhaps the key to the power of these sermons is best caught by a Union Seminary student's now legendary comment, first about Tillich's theological lectures and then about his sermons: 'We aren't sure we understand him; but he certainly understands us.' The 'we', of course, was quite specifically a mid twentieth-century northern hemisphere 'we'. However, the sense of being profoundly understood by this preacher is as powerful now as it was then. Readers today discover that these meditations illumine spiritual struggles that are perfectly familiar in the most ordinary moments of our lives. Tillich always insisted that Christianity has to be understood in terms of the concrete particularities of everyday life, and it was a major part of his genius to be able to bring to light religious dimensions embedded *in* such particularities rather than floating above them in abstract universality.

'The eternal now' is an image for eternity frequently used in the mystical tradition. Tillich would not have considered himself a 'mystic', but he did insist that there is a mystical aspect or dimension to ordinary experience. This collection of sermons focuses in particular on issues raised by the most ordinary of everyday experiences: awareness of the passage of time. First comes a set of meditations on the ways in which we experience the passage of time in everyday life as a threat and how our devices to fend off those threats tie us in binds. Second is a set of reflections on ways in which the very same experiences also include moments that can fairly be described as the presence of the Divine. Finally there is a set of meditations on the characteristics of a life lived in conscious response to that spiritual presence.

The power of these meditations does not require any knowledge of Tillich's systematic theology. They stand on their own. All they ask is a quiet spirit and a little time in which to live with them. They do not offer easy answers or sound-bite analyses of the human condition, but they do offer fresh ways of looking at your life and stimulation for your own religious reflection.

On the other hand, it is my experience that Tillich's three-volume *Systematic Theology* does not stand so well on its own. Tillich has to be counted as one of the three or four intellectually most powerful and religiously most profound systematic Christian thinkers in the last century and a half. But the conceptual complexity, intricate intellectual architecture and relentless abstraction of his *Systematic Theology* are so daunting that the Union student has a great deal of company in saying 'We're not sure we understand him'! It is a very great help in getting a concrete sense of just what Tillich is talking about to read the three volumes of his System in the light of the three volumes of his sermons. Of these three, *The Eternal Now* correlates with the culminating third volume of the System. There Tillich focuses on what he calls the 'Spiritual Presence' in the midst not only of religious search but of apparently secular human struggles with moral questions and cultural creativity.

Thus collections of Tillich's sermons such as *The Eternal Now* can serve as both entrance and exit to his System. As entrance, they can help ground the abstractions of the System in concrete experience. As exit, they can help illumine the practical upshot of the System for the shape of our daily lives. But serving as entrance or exit to Tillich's systematic thought is at most a secondary gain from reading *The Eternal Now*. It rewards reading for its own sake simply because it deepens us.

David H. Kelsey
Luther Wiegle Professor of Theology
Yale Divinity School

I

The Human Predicament

I

Loneliness and Solitude

And when he had sent the multitudes away, he went up into a mountain apart to pray: and when the evening was come, he was there alone.

MATT. 14.23

I

'He was there, alone.' So are we. Man is alone because he is man! In some way every creature is alone. In majestic isolation every star travels through the darkness of endless space. Each tree grows according to its own law, fulfilling its unique possibilities. Animals live, fight and die for themselves alone, confined to the limitations of their bodies. Certainly, they also appear as male and female, in families and in flocks. Some of them are gregarious. But all of them are alone! Being alive means being in a body – a body separated from all other bodies. And being separated means being alone.

This is true of every creature, and it is more true of man than of any other creature. He is not only alone; he also *knows* that he is alone. Aware of what he is, he asks the question of his aloneness. He asks why he is alone, and how he can triumph over his being alone. For this aloneness he cannot endure. Neither can he escape it. It is his destiny to be alone and to be aware of it. Not even God can take this destiny away from him.

In the story of paradise we read: 'Then the Lord God said, It is not good that man should be alone.' And he created the woman from the body of Adam. Here an old myth is used to show that originally there was no bodily separation between man and woman;

in the beginning they were one. Now they long to be one again. But although they recognize each other as flesh of their own flesh, each remains alone. They look at each other, and despite their longing for each other, they see their strangeness. In the story, God himself makes them aware of this fact when he speaks to each of them separately, when he makes each one responsible for his own guilt, when he listens to their excuses and mutual accusations, when he pronounces a separate curse over each, and leaves them to experience shame in the face of their nakedness. They are each alone. The creation of the woman has not overcome the situation which God describes as not good for man. He remains alone. And the creation of the woman, although it provides a helper for Adam, has only presented to the one human being who is alone another human being who is equally alone, and from their flesh all other men, each of whom will also stand alone.

We ask, however – is this really so? Did not God accomplish something better? Isn't our aloneness largely removed in the encounter of the sexes? Certainly it is during hours of communion and in moments of love. The ecstasy of love can absorb one's own self in its union with the other self, and separation seems to be overcome. But after these moments, the isolation of self from self is felt even more deeply than before, sometimes even to the point of mutual repulsion. We have given too much of ourselves, and now we long to take back what was given. Our desire to protect our aloneness is expressed in the feeling of shame. We feel ashamed when our intimate self, mental or bodily, is opened. We try to cover our nakedness, as did Adam and Eve when they became conscious of themselves. Thus, man and woman remain alone even in the most intimate union. They cannot penetrate each other's innermost centre. And if this were not so, they could not be helpers to each other; they could not have human community.

This is why God himself cannot liberate man from his aloneness: it is man's greatness that he is centred within himself. Separated from his world, he is thus able to look *at* it. Only because he can look at it can he know and love and transform it. God, in creating him the ruler of the earth, had to separate him and thrust him into aloneness. Man is also therefore able to be spoken to by God and by man. He can ask questions and give answers and make decisions. He has the freedom for good or evil. Only he who has an impenetrable centre in himself is free. Only he who is alone can claim to be a man. This is the greatness and this is the burden of man.

II

Our language has wisely sensed those two sides of man's being alone. It has created the word 'loneliness' to express the pain of being alone. And it has created the word 'solitude' to express the glory of being alone. Although, in daily life, we do not always distinguish between these words, we should do so consistently and thus deepen our understanding of our human predicament.

In the twenty-fifth Psalm we read: 'Turn thou to me and be gracious; for I am lonely and afflicted.' The psalmist feels the pain of loneliness. We do not know the character of his particular loneliness, but we know the many faces that loneliness can have. We have all experienced some of them.

Most widespread is our loneliness after those who helped us to forget that we are alone have left us, either through separation or death. I refer not only to those nearest to us, but also to those human beings who give us the feeling of communion, groups with which we have worked, with which we have had social contact, with which we have had spiritual communication. For many people such loneliness becomes a permanent state and a continuous source of profound melancholy. The sighing of innumerable lonely people, all around us and over the world, fills the ears that are opened by love.

But let us also consider those among us who are surrounded by friends and neighbours, by co-workers and countrymen, who live in family groups and enjoy the communion of the sexes – everything that those others do *not* have. And let us ask – are they without the pain of loneliness? Is their aloneness covered up by the crowd in which they move? If we can number ourselves among these people, we might answer the question as follows: I never felt so lonely as in that particular hour when I was surrounded by people but suddenly realized my ultimate isolation. I became silent and retired from the group in order to be alone with my loneliness. I wanted my external predicament to match my internal one. Let us not minimize such an experience by asserting that some people are simply not strong enough to obtain a significant place in the group, and that their withdrawal is nothing but an expression of weakness that may call for counselling or psychiatric help. Certainly, such people do exist in large numbers, and they need help. But I speak now of the strong ones, who have achieved their place in the crowd, and who nevertheless experience the terror of ultimate loneliness. They are aware, in a sudden break through the world around them, of man's real predicament. Let us also not minimize this experience by pointing out the fact that some people feel misunderstood despite their urgent desire to make themselves understandable, and therefore feel lonely in the crowd. No one can deny that there are such people and, further, that they even demonstrate a certain truth – for who is really understood, even by himself? The mystery of a person cannot be encompassed by a neat description of his character. Those, however, who always feel misunderstood confuse the mystery of each personality with imaginary treasures which they themselves believe they possess and which demand recognition from others. When such recognition is not forthcoming, they feel lonely and withdraw. They also need help. But again, there are those whose real treasures are great enough to find expression, to be understood and received, and yet who have this terrifying experience of ultimate loneliness. In such moments they break through the surface of their average life into the depth of man's predicament.

Many feel lonely because, in spite of their effort to love and be loved, their love is rejected. This loneliness is often self-created. These people may be claiming as a right what can only come to them as a gift. They withdraw into a self-chosen loneliness, taking revenge through bitterness and hostility towards those they feel have rejected them, actually enjoying the pain of their loneliness. There are many such persons, and they contribute heavily to the growth of neurotic loneliness in our time. They above all need help, for they easily become the prey of a demonic force that secludes them completely within themselves.

But there is also the genuine experience of rejected love. No special claim is made, but hope yearns towards another, and is disappointed. A community of love comes to an end or fails to exist at all. Such loneliness cuts our ties with the world. We are indeed ultimately alone, and not even love from other directions or the power of our own love can lift this burden from us. He who can endure the loneliness of disappointed love without bitterness experiences the depth of man's predicament radically and creatively.

There are, finally, two forms of loneliness that cannot either be covered or escaped: the loneliness of guilt and the loneliness of death. Nobody can remove from us what we have committed against our true being. We feel both our hidden guilt and our open guilt as *ours*, and ours alone. We cannot really make anybody else responsible for what we have done. We cannot run away from our guilt, and we cannot honestly cover it up. We are alone with it. And it is a loneliness that permeates all other forms of loneliness, transforming them into experiences of judgment.

Then, there is that ultimate loneliness of having to die. In the anticipation of our death we remain alone. No communication with others can remove it, as no other's presence in the actual hour of our dying can conceal the fact that it is *our* death, and our death alone. In the hour of death we are cut off from the whole universe and everything in it. We are deprived of all the things and beings that made us forget our being alone. Who can endure this loneliness?

III

Loneliness can be conquered only by those who can bear solitude. We have a natural desire for solitude because we are men. We want to feel what we are – namely, alone – not in pain and horror, but with joy and courage. There are many ways in which solitude can be sought and experienced. And each way can be called 'religious', if it is true, as one philosopher said, that 'religion is what a man does with his solitariness'.

One of these ways is the desire towards the silence of nature. We can speak without voice to the trees and the clouds and the waves of the sea. Without words they respond through the rustling of leaves and the moving of clouds and the murmuring of the sea. This solitude we can have, but only for a brief time. For we realize that the voices of nature cannot ultimately answer the questions in our mind. Our solitude in nature can easily become loneliness, and so we return to the world of man.

Solitude can also be found in the reading of poetry, in listening to music, in looking at pictures, and in sincere thoughtfulness. We are alone, perhaps in the midst of multitudes, but we are not lonely. Solitude protects us without isolating us. But life calls us back to its empty talk and the unavoidable demands of daily routine. It calls us back to its loneliness and the cover that it, in turn, spreads over our loneliness.

Without a doubt, this last describes not only man's general predicament, but also, and emphatically, our time. Today, more intensely than in preceding periods, man is so lonely that he cannot bear solitude. And he tries desperately to become a part of the crowd. Everything in our world supports him. It is a symptom of our disease that teachers and parents and the managers of public communication do everything possible to deprive us of the external conditions for solitude, the simplest aids to privacy. Even our houses, instead of protecting the solitude of each member of the family or group, are constructed to exclude privacy almost completely. The same holds true of the forms of communal life, the school, college, office and factory. An unceasing pressure attempts to destroy even our desire for solitude.

But sometimes God thrusts us out of the crowd into a solitude we did not desire, but which none the less takes hold of us. The prophet Jeremiah says – 'I sit alone, because thy hand was upon me'. God sometimes lays hands upon us. He wants us to ask the question of truth that may isolate us from most men, and that can be asked only in solitude. He wants us to ask the question of justice that may bring us suffering and death, and that can grow in us only in solitude. He wants us to break through the ordinary ways of men that may bring disrepute and hatred upon us, a breakthrough that can happen only in solitude. He wants us to penetrate to the boundaries of our being, where the mystery of life appears, and it can only appear in moments of solitude.

There may be some among you who long to become creative in some realm of life. But you cannot become or remain creative without solitude. One hour of conscious solitude will enrich your creativity far more than hours of trying to learn the creative process.

What happens in our solitude? Listen to Mark's words about Jesus' solitude in the desert – 'And he was in the wilderness forty days, tempted by Satan; and he was with the wild beasts, and the angels ministered to him.' He is alone, facing the whole earth and sky, the wild beasts around him and within him, he himself the battlefield for divine and demonic forces. So, first, this is what happens in our solitude: we meet ourselves, not as ourselves, but as the battlefield for creation and destruction, for God and the demons. Solitude is not easy. Who can bear it? It was not easy even for Jesus. We read: 'He went up into the hills to pray. When evening came, he was there alone.' When evening comes, loneliness becomes more lonely. We feel this when a day, or a period, or all the days of our life come to an end. Jesus went up to pray. Is this the way to transform loneliness into solitude and to bear solitude? It is not a simple question to answer. Most prayers do not have this much power. Most prayers make God a partner in a conversation; we use him to escape the only true way to solitude. Such prayers flow easily from the mouths of both ministers and laymen. But they are not born out of a solitary encounter of God with men. They are certainly not the kind of prayer for which Jesus went up into the hills. Better that we remain silent and allow our soul, that is always longing for solitude, to sigh without words to God. This we can do, even in a crowded day and a crowded room, even under the most difficult external conditions. This can give us moments of solitude that no one can take from us.

In these moments of solitude something is done to us. The centre of our being, the innermost self that is the ground of our aloneness, is elevated to the divine centre and taken into it. Therein can we rest without losing ourselves.

Now perhaps we can answer a question you may have already asked – how can communion grow out of solitude? We have seen that we can never reach the innermost centre of another being. We are always alone, each for himself. But we can reach it in a movement that rises first to God and then returns from him to the other self. In this way man's aloneness is not removed, but taken into the community with that in which the centres of all beings rest, and so into community with all of them. Even love is reborn in solitude. For only in solitude are those who are alone able to reach those from whom they are separated. Only the presence of the eternal can break through the walls that isolate the temporal from the temporal. One hour of solitude may bring us closer to those we love than many hours of communication. We can take them with us to the hills of eternity.

And perhaps when we ask – what is the innermost nature of solitude? – we should answer: the presence of the eternal upon the crowded roads of the temporal. It is the experience of being alone but not lonely, in view of the eternal presence that shines through the face of the Christ, and that includes everybody and everything from which we are separated. In the poverty of solitude all riches are present. Let us dare to have solitude – to face the eternal, to find others, to see ourselves.

2

Forgetting and Being Forgotten

One thing I do, forgetting what lies behind and straining forward to what lies ahead.

PHIL. 3.13

These very personal words of Paul, which appear in one of his most personal letters, lead us to ask – what did he want to forget? What do we forget, and what do we remember? What is the function of forgetting in man's life and in the household of the universe? Above all, what *should* we remember and what *should* we forget?

But in raising these questions, another more disturbing one comes to mind: what does it mean for a thing, for a being, to *be* forgotten? What does it mean for us when we *are* forgotten, in parts of our being, or totally, for a period, or for life? What does the thought that we may be forgotten in eternity do to us? How can we endure the words of the preacher when he says of the dead that 'the memory of them is dead', that they are forgotten 'with their love and their hate', and, according to the psalm, that their place knows them no more?

The simple word 'forget' can plunge us into the deepest riddles of life and death, of time and eternity. The Bible abounds in its use. For forgetting and remembering are two of the most astonishing qualities by which the divine image in man is made manifest. I ask you now to concentrate with me on the mystery of forgetting and remembering and of being forgotten, knowing in advance how limited our words and insights and courage must be in the face of such a mystery. Let us first consider forgetting and remembering, and then being forgotten and perhaps also being remembered.

I

Life could not continue without throwing the past into the past, liberating the present from its burden. Without this power life would be without a future; it would be enslaved by the past. Nothing new could happen; and even the old could not be, for what is now old was once something new, that might or might not have come into existence. Life, without pushing the past into the past, would be altogether impossible. But life has this power, as we are able to observe in the growth of every plant and of every animal. The earlier stages in the development of a living being are left behind in order to provide space for the future, for a new life. But not everything of the past is pushed into the past; something of the past remains alive in the present, so that there is ground from which to grow into the future. Every growth displays its conquered past, sometimes in the form of scars. Life uses its past and battles against it at the same time, in order to thrust forward towards its own renewal. In this pattern, man is united with all beings. It is the universal character of life, whether living beings are aware of it or not.

Only man can be fully aware of it. He saves the past by remembering it, and he pushes it back by forgetting it. This is the way that every child grows, both physically and in spirit. He preserves and he leaves behind. He remembers and he forgets. In healthy development, the balance between the two enables him to advance towards the new. But if too much is preserved, and too little forgotten, the way is barred: the past, with its infantile forces and memories, overpowers the future. We know that some of this occurs in the recesses of the inner life of all of us. We discover remnants of infancy that were never pushed into the past, where they belong. They constrict our freedom and narrow our path into the future. They may even produce a distortion of growth. Think of the preservation of infantile habits in our action and language: our adolescent withdrawal and aggression; the early images of ourselves and our world, far removed from reality; unfounded anxieties and foolish desires; a yet unshaken dependence on childhood authorities – father or mother; and our unquestioned prejudices that have no connection with our present stage of growth. There were occasions in the past when we lacked the strength to leave behind what belonged to the past; we forgot what belonged to oblivion. We forgot to forget, and now we may find it too late.

There have been nations that were unable to throw anything of their heritage into the past, and thus cut themselves off from new growth, until the weight of their past crushed their present and brought them to extinction. And sometimes we might ask if the Christian Church, as well as foreign religions, has not carried with it too much of its past, and left behind too little. Forgetting is probably more difficult for a religious tradition than any other human heritage. But God is not only the beginning from which we came; he is also the end to which we go. He is the creator of the *new* as well as the ancient of days. To all creatures he has given presence; and presence, although it rests on the past, drives into the future. Therefore, all life has received the gift of forgetting. A church that does not accept this gift denies its own creatureliness, and falls into the temptation of every church, which is to make itself God. Of course, no church or nation or person should ever forget its own identity. We are not asked to forget our name, the symbol of our inner self. And certainly, no church is required to forget its foundation. But if it is unable to leave behind much of what was built on this foundation, it will lose its future.

But all life, including man, not only leaves behind. It also preserves. It not only forgets. It also remembers. And the inability to remember is just as destructive as the inability to forget. An aged tree demonstrates that the life force of its original seed, which determined its final form, still exists. An animal would perish if it forgot the adjustments to life it learned from its first hour. The same is true of the human infant; and it is true of all his later growth in body and mind. Remembrance of the past preserves the identity of a human being with himself. Without it, he himself would be left behind by himself. This applies equally to all social groups. A formless rushing ahead, indiscriminate severing of the roots of the past, results in emptiness, a lack of presence, and thus, also, a lack of future. There are churches that, in their desire to forget, have lost the memory of their origins. There are nations that have cut themselves off from their traditions.

Perhaps one of the most conspicuous examples is our own nation, which has used a whole ocean as the drug of forgetfulness with respect to the sources of the civilization to which it belongs – Jerusalem and Athens. I do not speak of the scholarly knowledge of the past, of which there is no lack, but rather of the pushing forward of this nation into a future in which the creative forces of the past no longer exist. More than any other, our nation possesses the great power of forgetting. But this power is not balanced equally with the power of remembering, a fact that might become our undoing, spiritually and even politically. For if we lose our identity, we are lost.

II

We have considered forgetting a way in which life drives towards its own renewal. What and how do we forget? What did Paul forget, when he strained forward to what lay ahead? Obviously, he longed to forget his past as a Pharisee and a persecutor of Christianity. But every word of his letters proves that he never forgot.

There seem to be different kinds of forgetting. There is the natural forgetting of yesterday and most of the things that happened in it. If reminded, we might still remember some of them; but, slowly, even they tend to disappear. The whole day disappears, and only what was really significant in it is remembered. So most of the days of our lives vanish in forgetfulness. This natural process of forgetting operates without our co-operation, like the circulation of our blood.

But there is another aspect of forgetting that is familiar to us all. Something in us prevents us from remembering, when remembering proves to be too difficult or painful. We forget benefits, because the burden of gratitude is too heavy for us. We forget former loves, because the burden of obligations implied by them surpasses our strength. We forget former hates, because the task of nourishing them would disrupt our mind. We forget former pain, because it is still too painful. We forget former guilt, because we cannot endure its sting. Such forgetting is not the natural, daily form of forgetting.

It demands our co-operation. We repress what we cannot stand. We forget it by entombing it within us. Ordinary forgetting liberates us from innumerable small things in a natural process. Forgetting by repression does not liberate us, but seems to cut us off from what makes us suffer. We are not entirely successful, however, because the memory is buried within us, and influences every moment of our growth. And sometimes it breaks through its prison and strikes at us directly and painfully.

Then there is a forgetting, to which Paul witnesses, that liberates us not from the memory of past guilt but from the pain it brings. The grand old name for this kind of forgetting is repentance. Today, repentance is associated with a half-painful, half-voluptuous emotional concentration on one's guilt, and not with a liberating forgetfulness. But originally it meant a 'turning around', leaving behind the wrong way and turning towards the right. It means pushing the consciousness and pain of guilt into the past, not by repressing it, but by acknowledging it, and receiving the word of acceptance in spite of it. If we are able to repent, we are able to forget, not because the forgotten act was unimportant, and not because we repress what we cannot endure, but because we have acknowledged our guilt and can now live with it. For it is *eternally* forgotten. This was how Paul forgot what lay behind him, although it always remained with him.

This kind of forgetting is decisive for our personal relationships. None of them is possible without a silent act of forgiving, repeated again and again. Forgiving presupposes remembering. And it creates a forgetting not in the natural way we forget yesterday's weather, but in the way of the great 'in spite of' that says: I forget although I remember. Without this kind of forgetting no human relationship could endure healthily. I don't refer to a solemn act of asking for and offering forgiveness. Such rituals as sometimes occur between parents and children, or friends, or man and wife, are often acts of moral arrogance on the one part and enforced humiliation on the other. But I speak of the lasting willingness to accept him who has hurt us. Such forgiveness is the highest form of forgetting, although it is not forgetfulness. The stumbling block of having violated another is pushed into the past, and there is the possibility of something new in the relationship.

Forgetting in spite of remembering is forgiveness. We can *live* only because our guilt is forgiven and thus *eternally* forgotten. And we can love only because we forgive and are forgiven.

III

Paul is straining to what lies ahead. What does lie ahead? When we ask this question, we are reminded of quite another kind of forgetting, forgetting that someday we shall be forgotten. Since we cannot endure the thought we repress it. The literature of mankind is full of stories in which kings as well as beggars are reminded of their having to die. Man cannot stand the anticipation of death, and so he represses it. But the repression does not remove his ever-present anxiety, and there are moments in the life of everyone when such repression is not even slightly effective. Then, we ask ourselves – will there be a time when I shall be forgotten, forever? The meaning of the anxiety of having to die is the anxiety that one will be forgotten both now and in eternity. Every living being resists being pushed into the past without a new presence. A powerful symbol of this state of being forgotten is being buried. Burial means being removed from the realm of awareness, a removal from the surface of the earth. The meaning of Jesus' resurrection is intensified by the words in the Creed that he 'was buried'.

A rather superficial view of the anxiety of death states that this anxiety is the fear of the actual process of dying, which of course may be agonizing, but which can also be very easy. No, in the depth of the anxiety of having to die is the anxiety of being eternally forgotten.

Man was never able to bear this thought. An expression of his utter resistance is the way the Greeks spoke of glory as the conquest of being forgotten. Today, the same thing is called 'historical significance'. If one can, one builds memorial halls or creates memorial foundations. It is consoling to think that we might be remembered for a certain time beyond death not only by those who loved us or hated us or admired us, but also by those who never knew us except now by name. Some names are remembered for centuries. Hope is expressed in the poet's proud assertion that 'the traces of his earthly days cannot vanish in aeons'. But these traces, which unquestionably exist in the physical world, are not we ourselves, and they don't bear our name. They do not keep us from being forgotten.

Is there anything that can keep us from being forgotten? That we were known from eternity and will be remembered in eternity is the only certainty that can save us from the horror of being forgotten forever. We cannot be forgotten because we are known eternally, beyond past and future.

But, although we cannot be forgotten, we can forget ourselves – namely, our true being, that part of us that is eternally known and eternally remembered. And whether or not we forget or remember most of those things we experience every hour is not ultimately important. But it is infinitely important that we do not forget ourselves, this individual being, not to be repeated, unique, eternally precious, and delivered into our hands. Unfortunately, it may then be mistreated, overlooked, and imprisoned. Yet, if we remember it, and become aware of its infinite significance, we realize that we have been known in the past and that we will not be forgotten in the future. For the truth of our own being is rooted in the ground of being, from which it comes and to which it returns.

Nothing truly real is forgotten eternally, because everything real comes from eternity and goes to eternity. And I speak now of all individual men and not solely of man. Nothing in the universe is unknown, nothing real is ultimately forgotten. The atom that moves in an immeasurable path today and the atom that moved in an immeasurable path billions of years ago are rooted in the eternal ground. There is no absolute, no completely forgotten past, because the past, like the future, is rooted in the divine life. Nothing is completely pushed into the past. Nothing real is absolutely lost and forgotten. We are together with everything real in the divine life. Only the unreal, in us and around us, is pushed into the past forever. This is what 'last judgment' means – to separate in us, as in everything, what has true and final being from what is merely transitory and empty of true being. We are never forgotten, but much in us that we liked and for which we longed may be forgotten forever. Such judgment goes on in every moment of our lives, but the process is hidden in time and manifest only in eternity. Therefore, let us push into the past and forget what should be forgotten forever, and let us go forward to that which expresses our true being and cannot be lost in eternity.

3

The Riddle of Inequality

For to him who has will more be given; and from him who has not, even what he has will be taken away.

MARK 4.25

One day a learned colleague called me up and cried angrily, 'There is a saying in the New Testament which I consider to be one of the most immoral and unjust statements ever made!' And he began to quote our text – 'To him who has will more be given', his anger increasing as he continued, 'and from him who has not, *even what he has will be taken away.*' I believe that most of us cannot but feel equally offended. And we cannot easily excuse the passage by suggesting what this colleague suggested – that the words may be due to a misunderstanding on the part of the disciples. No, they appear at least four times in the gospels with great emphasis. And furthermore, it is clear that the writers of the gospels feel exactly as we do. For them, the statement is a stumbling block, and they tried to interpret it in different ways. Probably none of the explanations satisfied them fully, for this particular saying of Jesus confronts us immediately with the greatest and perhaps most painful riddle of life – the inequality of all beings. We certainly cannot hope to solve it. Neither the Bible nor any of the great religions and philosophies was able to do so. But this we can do: we can explore the breadth and depth of the riddle of inequality; and we can try to find a way to live with it, unsolved as it may remain.

I

When we consider the words, 'to him who has will more be given', we ask ourselves – what *do* we have? And we may discover that much has been given us in terms of external goods, of friends, of intellectual gifts, and even of a comparatively high morality on which to base our action. So we can expect that even more will accrue to us, while, at the same time, those who are lacking in all these attributes will lose the little they already have. Even further, according to Jesus' parable, the one poor talent they possess shall be handed over to those who have five or ten talents. We shall be richer because they will be poorer. And cry out as we may against such an injustice, we cannot deny that life abounds in it. We cannot deny it, but we might well ask – do we really *have* what we believe we have, so that it cannot be taken from us? It is a question full of anxiety, intensified by Luke's version of our text: 'From him who has not, even what he *thinks* that he has will be taken away.' Perhaps our having of those many things is not the kind of having that can be increased. Perhaps the having of a few things on the part of the poor is the kind of having that makes them grow. Jesus confirms this thought in the parable of the talents. The talents that are used, at the risk of their being lost, are the talents that we really have. Those that we try to preserve, without risking their use for growth, are those that we do not really have, and that will therefore be taken from us. They begin to disappear, until suddenly we feel that we have lost them, perhaps forever.

Let us apply the principle to our own life, be it long or short. In the memory of all of us, there are many things that we seemed to have, but that we really did *not* have, and that were therefore taken away from us. Some of them were lost because of the tragic limitations of life. They had to be sacrificed so that other things might grow. We were all given childish innocence, but innocence cannot be used and increased. The growth of our lives is made possible only by the sacrifice of the original gift of innocence. Sometimes, nevertheless, a melancholy longing arises in us for a purity that has been taken from us. We were all given youthful enthusiasm for many things and goals. But all this enthusiasm also cannot be used and increased. Most of the objects of our early enthusiasm must be sacrificed for a few, and those few approached soberly. No maturity is possible without this sacrifice. Yet often a deep yearning for the lost possibilities and that enthusiasm takes hold of us. Innocence and youthful enthusiasm: we had them, and we did not have them. Life itself demanded that they be taken from us.

But there are other things that we had and that were taken from us because we were guilty of taking them too much for granted. Some of us were deeply sensitive to the wonder of life as it is revealed in nature. Slowly, under the pressure of work and social life and the lure of cheap pleasures, we lost the wonder of our earlier years – the intense joy and sense of the mystery of life in the freshness of the young day or the glory of the dying afternoon, the splendour of the mountains and the infinity of the sea, or in the perfection of the movements of a young animal or of a flower breaking through the soil. We try perhaps to evoke such feelings again, but we find ourselves empty and do not succeed. We had that sensitivity and we did not have it, and it was taken from us.

Others of us have had the same experience with respect to music, poetry, great literature and the drama. We desired to devour all of these; we lived in them, and through them created for ourselves a life beyond our daily life. We had this experience and we did not have it. We did not allow it to grow. Our love for it was not strong enough, and so it was taken from us.

Many people remember a time when the desire to solve the riddles of the universe and to find *truth* was the driving force in their lives. They entered college and the university not in order to gain access to the upper middle classes or the preconditions for social and economic success, but because they felt driven by their thirst for knowledge. They had something to which, seemingly, more could be added. But their desire was not strong enough. They failed to nurture it, and so it was taken from them. Expediency and indifference towards truth took the place of genuine academic interest. Because their love for the truth was let go, they sometimes feel sick at heart; they realize that what they have lost may never be returned to them.

We all know that any deep relationship to another human being requires watchfulness and nourishment; otherwise, it is taken from us. And we cannot recapture it. This is a form of having and not having that is the root of innumerable human tragedies. We are all familiar with them.

And there is the most fundamental kind of having and not having – our having and losing God. Perhaps in our childhood, and even beyond it, our experience of God was rich. We may remember the moments in which we felt his presence intensely. We may remember our praying with an overflowing heart, our encounter with the holy in words and music and holy places. We communicated with God; but this communication was taken from us, because we had it and did not have it. We failed to let it grow, and therefore, it slowly disappeared, leaving only an empty space. We became unconcerned, cynical and indifferent, not because we doubted our religious traditions – such doubt belongs to a life rich in God – but because we turned away from what once concerned us infinitely.

Such thoughts mark the first step in approaching the riddle of inequality. Those who have receive more if they *really* have what they have, if they use it and cause it to grow. And those who have not lose what they seem to have, because they really do *not* have.

II

But the question of inequality has not yet been answered. For now we must ask – why do some of us receive more than others in the very beginning, before using or wasting our talents is even possible? Why does the one servant receive five talents, and the second, two, and the third, one? Why is one person born to desperate poverty, and another to affluence? To reply that much will be demanded of those to whom much is given, and little of those to whom little is given, is not adequate. For it is just this original inequality, internal and external, that gives rise to the question. Why is the power to gain so much more out of his being human given to one human being rather than to another? Why is so much given to one that much *can* be asked of him, while little can be asked of another, because little was given him? If we consider this problem in relation not only to individual men, but also to classes, races and nations, the question of political inequality also arises, and with it the many ways in which men have tried to abolish inequality. In every revolution and war, the will to solve the riddle of inequality is a driving force. But neither war nor revolution can answer it. And even though we may imagine that most social inequalities will be conquered in the future, there remain three realities: the inequality of talents in body and mind, the inequality created by freedom and destiny, and the inequality of justice deriving from the fact that all generations before the time of such equality would by nature be excluded from its blessings. This last would be the greatest inequality possible! No! In the face of one of the deepest and most tormenting problems of life, we cannot permit ourselves to be so shallow or foolish as to try to escape into a social dreamland. We have to live now. We have to live *this* life. We must face the riddle of inequality today.

Let us not confuse the riddle of inequality with the fact that each of us is a unique and incomparable self. Our being individual certainly belongs to our dignity as men. This being was given to us, and must be made use of and intensified, not drowned in the gray waters of conformity that threaten us so much today. One should defend every individuality and the uniqueness of every human self. But one should not be deluded into believing that this is a solution to the riddle of inequality. Unfortunately, there are social and political reactionaries who exploit this confusion in order to justify social injustice. They are at least as foolish as those who dream of the future abolition of inequality. He who has witnessed hospitals for the ill and insane, prisons, sweat shops, battlefields, people starving, family tragedies, or moral aberrations, should be cured of any confusion of the gift of individuality with the riddle of inequality. He should be cured of any sense of easy consolation.

And now we must take the third step in our attempt to penetrate the riddle of inequality by asking – why do some of us use and increase what was given to us, while others do not and thus lose what was given them? Why does God say to the prophet in the Old Testament that the ears and eyes of a nation are made insensitive to the divine message? Is it sufficient to answer – because some use their freedom responsibly and do what they ought to do, while others fail through their own guilt? This answer, which seems so obvious, *is* sufficient only when we apply it to ourselves. Each one of us must consider the increase or loss of what was given as a matter for his own responsibility. Our conscience tells us that we cannot blame anybody or anything other than ourselves for our losses.

But when we consider the plight of others, this answer is *not* sufficient. We cannot tell somebody who comes to us in great distress about himself – 'Make use of what was given you', for he may have come to us precisely because he is unable to do so! And we cannot tell those in despair because of what they are – 'Be something else', for the inability to get rid of oneself is the exact meaning of despair. We cannot tell those who failed to conquer the destructive influences of their surroundings and thence were driven into crime and misery – 'You should have been stronger', for it was just this strength of which they were deprived by heritage or environment. Certainly they are all men, and freedom is given to them all. But they are also all subject to destiny. It is not for us to condemn others because they *were* free, as it is also not for us to excuse them because of the burden of their destiny. We cannot judge them. And when we judge ourselves, we must keep in mind that even this judgment has no finality, because we, like them, stand under an ultimate judgment. In it the riddle of inequality is eternally answered. But the answer is not ours. It is our predicament that we must ask the question, and we ask with an uneasy conscience – why are they in such misery? Why not we? Thinking of those near to us, we ask – are we partly responsible? But even though we are, the riddle of inequality is not solved. The uneasy conscience asks also about those most distant from us – why they, why not we?

Why did my child, or any one of millions of children, die before he had the chance to grow out of infancy? Why was my child, or any child, born crippled in mind or body? Why has my friend or relative, or anyone's friend or relative, disintegrated in his mind, and thus lost both his freedom and his destiny? Why has my son or daughter, gifted as they were with many talents, wasted them and been deprived of them? Why do such things happen to any parent at all? And why have the creative powers of this boy or that girl been broken by a tyrannical father or a possessive mother?

None of these questions concern our own misery. At present, we are not asking – why did this happen to me? It is not Job's question that God answered by humiliating him and then elevating him into communion with him. It is not the old and urgent question – where is divine justice, where is divine love, for me? It is almost an opposite question – why did this *not* happen to me, while it did happen to another, to innumerable other ones, to whom not even Job's power to accept the divine answer was given? Why, Jesus asks also, are many called but few elected? He does not answer the question, but states simply that this is the human predicament. Shall we therefore cease to ask, and humbly accept a divine judgment that would hurl most human beings out of community with the divine and condemn them to despair and self-destruction? Can we accept the eternal victory of judgment over love? We can *not*, nor can any human being, though he may preach and threaten in such terms. As long as he is unable to visualize himself with absolute certainty as eternally rejected, his preaching and threats are self-deceptive. For who can see himself eternally rejected?

But if this is not the solution of the riddle of inequality at its deepest level, may we go outside the boundaries of Christian tradition to listen to those who would tell us that this life does not determine our eternal destiny? There will be other lives, they would say, predicated, like our present life, on previous ones and what we wasted or achieved in them. This is a serious doctrine and not completely strange to Christianity. But since we do not know and never shall know what each of us was in a previous existence, or

will be in a future one, it is not really *our* destiny developing from
life to life, but in each life, the destiny of someone *else*. Therefore,
this doctrine also fails to solve the riddle of inequality.

Actually, there is no answer at all to our question concerning the
temporal and eternal destiny of a single being separated from the
destiny of the whole. Only in the unity of all beings in time and
eternity can there be a humanly possible answer to the riddle of
inequality. 'Humanly possible' does not mean an answer that
removes the riddle of inequality, but one with which we can live.

There is an ultimate unity of all beings, rooted in the divine life
from which they emerge and to which they return. All beings,
non-human as well as human, participate in it. And therefore they
all participate in each other. And we participate in each other's
having and in each other's not having. When we become aware of
this unity of all beings, something happens to us. The fact that
others do *not* have, changes the character of our having: it undercuts
our security and drives us beyond ourselves, to understand, to give,
to share, to help. The fact that others fall into sin, crime and misery,
alters the character of the grace that is given us: it makes us recognize
our own hidden guilt; it shows us that those who suffer for their
sin and crime suffer also for us, for we are guilty of their guilt and
ought to suffer as they suffer. Our becoming aware of the fact that
others who *could* have developed into full human beings did not
change our state of full humanity. Their early death, their early or
late disintegration, brings to our own personal life and health a
continuous risk, a dying that is not yet death, a disintegration that
is not yet destruction. In every death we encounter, something
of us dies, and in every disease, something of us tends towards
disintegration.

Can we live with this answer? We can, to the degree to which
we are liberated from seclusion in ourselves. But no one can be
liberated from himself unless he is grasped by that power which is
present in everyone and everything – the eternal, from which we
come and to which we go, and which gives us *to* ourselves and
liberates us *from* ourselves. It is the greatness and heart of the
Christian message that God, as manifest in the Christ on the Cross,
totally participates in the dying of a child, in the condemnation of

the criminal, in the disintegration of a mind, in starvation and famine, and even in the human rejection of himself. There is no human condition into which the divine presence does not penetrate. This is what the Cross, the most extreme of all human conditions, tells us. The riddle of inequality cannot be solved on the level of our separation from each other. It is eternally solved through the divine participation in the life of all of us and every being. The certainty of divine participation gives us the courage to endure the riddle of inequality, although our finite minds cannot solve it.

4

The Good that I will, I do not

For I do not do the good I want, but the evil I do not want is what I do. Now if I do what I do not want, it is no longer I that do it, but sin which dwells within me.

ROM. 7.19–20

'I do not do the good I want, but the evil I do not want is what I do.' Do these words of Paul correctly describe our nature? Is the split between willing the good and achieving it as radical as they would indicate? Or do we resist the indictment by insisting that we often do the good that we want and avoid the evil that we do not want? Is not Paul perhaps grossly exaggerating the evil in man in order to emphasize the brightness of grace by depicting it against a very dark background? These are questions that every critic of Christianity asks. But are they not also the questions that *we* ask – we, who call ourselves Christians, or at least who desire to be what the Christian message wills us to be? Actually, none of us believes that he *always* does the evil he would like not to do. We know that we sometimes do achieve the good that we want – when, for example, we perform an act of love towards a person with whom we do not sympathize, or an act of self-discipline for the sake of our work, or an act of courageous non-conformity in a situation where it may endanger us. Our moral balance sheet is not as bad as it would be without these acts! And have we ever really known a preacher of what is called 'the total depravity of man' who did not show, in his own behaviour, reliance on a positive moral balance sheet? Perhaps even Paul did. At least, he tries to tell us so when he boasts about his sufferings and activities in a letter to the Corinthians. Certainly, he calls his boasting foolishness. But do not we also insist that our boasting is foolish? Yet we do not stop boasting. Are not perhaps these who believe, on the surface, that they have nothing to boast about, being sick, disintegrated, and without self-esteem? They may even be proud of the depth of despair in which they visualize themselves. For without a vestige of self-esteem no one can live, not even he who bases his self-esteem on despairing of himself.

But why then do we not simply dismiss Paul's words? Why do we react positively to his statement that 'I do not do the good that I want'? It is because we feel that it is not a matter of balance sheets between good and evil that the words express, but rather a matter of our whole being, of our situation as men, of our standing in the face of the eternal – the source, aim and judge of our being. It is our human predicament that a power takes hold of us, that does not come from us but is in us, a power that we hate and at the same time gladly accept. We are fascinated by it; we play with it; we obey it. But we know that it will destroy us if we are not grasped by another power that will resist and control it. We are fascinated by what can destroy us, and in moments even feel a hidden desire to be destroyed by it. This is how Paul saw himself, and how a great many of us see ourselves.

People who call themselves Christian – parents, teachers, preachers – tell us that we should be 'good' and obey the will of God. For many of them the will of God is not very different from the will of those socially correct beings whose conventions they ask us to accept. If we only willed such goodness, they say, we could achieve it, and would be rewarded in time and eternity – but first of all, in time.

One can thank God that such preaching has become more and more suspect, for it does not strike at the real human situation. The eyes of many serious people in our time have been opened to an awareness of their predicament as men. Every sentence in Paul's message is directed against the so-called 'men of good will'. They are the very ones he sees as driven by some power to act against their good will. And they are *we*. For who amongst us is not full of good will? But perhaps if we come to know ourselves better, we may begin to suspect that some of this good will is not so good after all, and that we are driven by forces of which we might not even be aware.

It is not necessary to describe those who embody good will and work towards just the opposite on a level hidden beneath their goodness: Psychologists and others have done this so fully that it needs no repetition. Despite what critics have to say of our time, one of the great things to have come out of it is the difficulty of anyone's being able to hide permanently from himself and from others the motives for his actions. Whatever we may think about the methods employed to reach this insight, the insight itself is infinitely precious.

It has also become difficult for a man who works with dedication and success at his business or profession to feel assured about the goodness of what he is doing. He cannot hide from himself that his commitment to his work may also be a way of escaping genuine human commitments and, above all, a way of escaping himself.

And it has become difficult for a mother who loves her children passionately to be sure that she feels only love for them. She can no longer conceal from herself that her anxiety concerning their well-being may be an expression of her will to dominate them or a form of guilt for a heavily veiled hostility that desires to be rid of them.

And we cannot applaud every act of moral self-restraint, knowing that its cause may be cowardice preventing a revolution against inherited, though already questioned, rules of behaviour. Nor can we praise every act of daring nonconformism, knowing that its reason may be the inability of an individual to resist the persuasive irresponsibility of a group of nonconformists.

In these and countless other cases, we experience a power that dwells in us and directs our will against itself.

The name of this power is sin. Nothing is more precarious today than the mention of this word among Christians, as well as among non-Christians, for in everyone there is a tremendous resistance to it. It is a word that has fallen into disrepute. To some of us it sounds almost ridiculous and is apt to provoke laughter rather than serious consideration. To others, who take it more seriously, it implies an attack on their human dignity. And again, to others – those who have suffered from it – it means the threatening countenance of the disciplinarian, who forbids them to do what they would like and demands of them what they hate. Therefore, even Christian teachers, including myself, shy away from the use of the word sin. We know how many distorted images it can produce. We try to avoid it, or to substitute another word for it. But it has a strange quality. It always returns. We cannot escape it. It is as insistent as it is ugly. And so it would be more honest – and this I say to myself – to face it and ask what it really is.

It is certainly not what men of good will would have us believe – failure to act in the right way, a failure to do the good one should and could have done. If this were sin, a less aggressive and less ugly term, such as human weakness, could be applied. But that is just what sin is *not*. And those of us who have experienced demonic powers within and around ourselves find such a description ludicrous. So we turn to Paul, and perhaps to Dostoevski's Ivan Karamazov, or to the conversation between the devil and the hero in Thomas Mann's *Dr Faustus*. From them we learn what sin is. And perhaps we may learn it through Picasso's picture of that small Basque village, Guernica, which was destroyed in an unimaginably horrible way by the demonic powers of Fascism and Nazism. And perhaps we learn it through the disrupting sounds in music that does not bring us restful emotions, but the feeling of being torn and split. Perhaps we learn the meaning of sin from the images of evil and guilt that fill our theatres, or through the revelations of unconscious motives so abundant in our novels. It is noteworthy that today, in order to know the meaning of sin, we have to look outside our churches and their average preaching to the artists and writers and ask *them*. But perhaps there is still another place where we can learn what sin is, and that is our own heart.

Paul seldom speaks of sins, but he often speaks of Sin – Sin in the singular with a capital 'S', Sin as a power that controls world and mind, persons and nations.

Have you ever thought of Sin in this image? It is the biblical image. But how many Christians or non-Christians have seen it? Most of us remember that at home, in school and at church, we were taught that there were many things that one would like to do that one should not. And if one did them, one committed a sin. We also remember that we were told of things we should do, although we disliked doing them. And if we did not do them, we committed a sin. We had lists of prohibitions and catalogues of commands; if we did not follow them, we committed sins. Naturally, we did commit one or more sins every day, although we tried to diminish their number seriously and with good will. This was, and perhaps still is, our image of sin – a poor, petty, distorted image, and the reason for the disrepute into which the word has fallen.

The first step to an understanding of the Christian message that is called 'good news' is to dispel the image of sin that implies a catalogue of sins. Those who are bound to this image are also those who find it most difficult to receive the message of acceptance of the unacceptable, the good news of Christianity. Their half-sinfulness and half-righteousness makes them insensitive to a message that states the presence of total sinfulness and total righteousness in the same man at the same moment. They never find the courage to make a total judgment against themselves, and therefore, they can never find the courage to believe in a total acceptance of themselves.

Those, however, who have experienced in their hearts that sin is more than the trespassing of a list of rules, know that all sins are manifestations of Sin, of the power of estrangement and inner conflict. Sin dwells in us, it controls us, and makes us do what we don't want to do. It produces a split in us that makes us lose identity with ourselves. Paul writes of this split twice: 'If I do what I do not want, it is no longer I that do it, but sin which dwells within me.' Those who have suffered this split know how unexpected and terrifying it can be. Thoughts entered our mind, words poured from our mouth, something was enacted by us suddenly and without warning. And if we look at what happened, we feel – 'It could not have been *I* who acted like this. I cannot find myself in it. Something came upon me, something I hardly noticed. But there it was and here am I. It is *I* who did it, but a strange I. It is not my real, my innermost self. It is as though I were possessed by a power I scarcely knew. But now I know that it not only can reach me, but that it dwells in me.'

Is this something we really know? Or do we, after a moment of shock, repress such knowledge? Do we still rely on our comparatively well-ordered life, avoiding situations of moral danger, determined by the rules of family, school and society? For those who are satisfied with such a life, the words of Paul are written in vain. They refuse to face their human predicament. But something further may happen to them: God himself may throw them into more sin in order to make them aware of what they really are. This is a bold way of speaking, but it is the way people of the profoundest religious experiences have spoken. By his throwing them into more sin, they have felt the awakening hand of God. And awakened, they have seen themselves in the mirror from which they had always turned away. No longer able to hide from themselves, they have asked the question, from the depth of their self-rejection, to which the Christian message is the answer – the power of acceptance that can overcome the despair of self-rejection. In this sense, *more* sin can be the divine way of making us aware of ourselves.

Then, we ask with Paul – what is it within us that makes a dwelling place for this power? He answers that it is our members in which sin hides. He also calls this place 'flesh', and sometimes he speaks of 'our body of death'. But there are also forces within us that resist the power – our innermost self, our mind, our spirit. With these words, Paul wrestles with the deep mystery of human nature just as we do today. And it is no easier to understand him than our present scholarly language about man. But one thing is certain: Paul, and with him the whole Bible, never made our body responsible for our estrangement from God, from our world and from our own self. Body, flesh, members – these are not the only sinful part of us, while the innermost self, mind and spirit, comprises the other, sinless part. Our whole being, every cell of our body, and every movement of our mind is both flesh and spirit, subjected to the power of sin and resisting its power. The fact that we accuse ourselves proves that we still have an awareness of what we truly are, and therefore ought to be. And the fact that we excuse ourselves shows that we cannot acknowledge our estrangement from our true nature. The fact that we are ashamed shows that we still know what we ought to be.

There is no part of man that is bad in itself, as there is no part

The Eternal Now

of man that is good in itself. Any Christian teaching that has forgotten this has fallen short of the height of Christian insight. And here all Christian churches must share the grave guilt of destroying human beings by casting them into despair over their own guilt where there should be no guilt. In pulpits, schools and families, Christians have called the natural strivings of the living, growing and self-propagating body sinful. They concentrate in an inordinate and purely pagan way on the sexual differentiation of all life and its possible distortions. Certainly, these distortions are as real as the distortions of our spiritual life – as, for example, pride and indifference. But to see the power of sin in the sexual power of life as such is itself a distortion. Such preaching completely misses the image of sin as Paul depicts it. What is worse, it produces distorted feelings of guilt in countless personalities, that drive them from anxiety to despair, from despair to escape into mental disease, and thence the desire to destroy themselves altogether.

And still other consequences of this preaching about sin become apparent. Paul points to the perversion of sexual desires as an extreme expression of sin's control of mankind. Have we as Christians ever asked ourselves whether or not, in our defamation of the natural as sin, or at least as a reason for shame, we have perhaps contributed most potently to this state of affairs? For all this results from that petty image of sin, that contradicts reality as much as it contradicts the biblical understanding of man's predicament.

It is dangerous to preach about sin, because it may induce us to brood over our sinfulness. Perhaps one should not preach about it at all. I myself have hesitated for many years. But sometimes it must be risked in order to remove the distortions which increase sin, if, by the persistence of wrong thoughts, wrong ways of living are inevitable.

I believe it possible to conquer the dangers implied in the concentration on sin, if we look at it *indirectly*, in the light of that which enables us to resist it – reunion overcoming estrangement. Sin is our act of turning away from participation in the divine Ground from which we come and to which we go. Sin is the turning towards ourselves, and making ourselves the centre of our world and of ourselves. Sin is the drive in every one, even those who exercise the most self-restraint, to draw as much as possible of the world into oneself. But we can be fully aware of this only if we have found a certain level of life above ourselves. Whoever has found himself after he has lost himself knows how deep his loss of self was. If we look at our estrangement from the point of reunion, we are no longer in danger of brooding over our estrangement. We can speak of Sin, because its power over us is broken.

It is certainly not broken by ourselves. The attempt to break the power of sin by the power of good will has been described by Paul as the attempt to fulfil the law, the law in our mind, in our innermost self that is the law of God. The result of this attempt is failure, guilt and despair. The law, with its commands and prohibitions, despite its function in revealing and restricting evil, provokes resistance against itself. In a language both poetic and profoundly psychological, Paul says that the sin that dwells in our members is asleep until the moment in which it is awakened by the 'thou shalt not'. Sin uses the commandments in order to become alive. Prohibition awakens sleeping desire. It arouses the power and consciousness of sin, but cannot break its power. Only if we accept with our whole being the message that it *is* broken, is it also broken in us.

This picture of sin is a picture full of ugliness, suffering and shame, and, at the same time, drama and passion. It is the picture of us as the battleground of powers greater than we. It does not divide men into categories of black and white, or good and evil. It does not appear as the threatening finger of an authority urging us – do not sin! But it is the vision of something infinitely important, that happens on this small planet, in our bodies and minds. It raises mankind to a level in the universe where decisive things happen in every moment, decisive for the ultimate meaning of all existence. In each of us such decisions occur, in us, and through us. This is our burden. This is our despair. This is our greatness.

5

Heal the Sick; Cast out the Demons

Address to graduating students at
Union Theological Seminary, New York, 1955

Heal the sick; . . . cast out the demons.
MATT. 10.8

Members of the outgoing class! Friends!

The first difficulty you will experience when Jesus sends you ahead of him and gives you the power of healing is that many people will tell you that they do not need to be healed. And if you come to them with the claim that you will cast out the demons that rule their lives, they will laugh at you and assure you that *you* are possessed by a demon – just as they said to Jesus.

Therefore, the first task of a minister is to make men aware of their predicament. Many of those who have gone out from our seminary to various congregations and communities have despaired over this task. And they have either given up the ministry altogether, or they minister only to those who consider themselves healthy. They have forgotten that their task is to heal those who *are* sick, which includes those who are not aware that they are sick. There is no easy way to make them aware of their predicament. God, certainly, has his ways of doing so. He shakes the complacency of those who consider themselves healthy by hurling them, both externally and internally, into darkness and despair. He reveals to them what they are by splitting the foundations of their self-assurance. He reveals their blindness towards themselves. This *we* cannot achieve, not even for ourselves. But we can be open to the moment when it happens to us. And if it happens, we can become tools of the power that may heal others. To try this is the first task of the minister, and perhaps the hardest of them all. But you are not the only ones who are used as tools. Everyone is potentially a tool of healing for anyone else. And it often happens that healing power works outside the Church and the ministry. The fact that Jesus gave the disciples responsibility for healing and casting out demons does not constitute a special prerogative on the part of the minister. Every Christian receives this charge, and each of us should take it seriously in our relation to one another. Everyone should accept his priestly responsibility for everyone else. The minister has no magic power to heal. Even his administration of the liturgy and sacraments does not give him this power. But in his special vocation, he stands for the universal power given to the Church to heal and to cast out demons.

Why have these assertions, that were so central at the time the gospel was first preached, lost their significance in our own period? The reason, I believe, lies in the words 'healing' and 'casting out demons', that have been misunderstood as miracle-healing, based on magic power and magic self-suggestion. There is no doubt that such phenomena occur. They happen here, and everywhere else in the world. They happen and are used in the midst of Christianity. But the Church was right when it felt that this was not the task of the Church and its ministers. It is an abuse of the name of the Christ to use it as a magic formula. Nevertheless, the words of our text remain valid. They belong to the message of the Christ, and they tell us about something that belongs to the Christ as the Christ – the power to conquer the demonic forces that control our lives, mind and body. And I believe that, of all the different ways to communicate the message of the Christ to others, this way will prove to be the most adequate for the people of our time. It is something they can understand. For in every country of the world, including our own, there is an awareness of the power of evil that has not existed for centuries. If we look at our period as a whole, we realize that not only special groups fall under the judgment of Jesus' ironic words – 'Those who are well have no need of a physican, but those who are sick'. In spite of the many who resist this insight, we know that we are sick, that we are not whole. The central message for our contemporaries, including ourselves, the message awaited by many both within and outside our congregations is the good news of the healing power that is in the world and whose expression is the Christ.

The task of healing demands of you insight into the nature of life and the human situation. People often ask, in passionate despair, why the divine order of things includes sickness, if sickness is one of the things to be healed by divine order. This very natural question, which, for many of us, is *the* stumbling block of our faith, points to the riddle of evil in the world of God. You will have to deal with this question more often than with any other. And you must not avoid the question by retiring behind the term 'mystery'. Of course, there is mystery – divine mystery – and in contrast to it, the mystery of evil. But it belongs to the insights demanded of you that you put the mystery in its right place, and explain what can and must be explained. Evil in the divine order is not only mystery; it is also revelation. It reveals the greatness and danger of life. He who can become sick is greater than he who cannot, than that which is bound to remain what it is, unable to be split in itself. He alone who is free is able to surrender to the demonic forces that turn his freedom into bondage. The gift of freedom implies the danger of servitude; and the abundance of life implies the danger of sickness. Man's life is abundant life, infinitely complex, inexhaustible in its possibilities, even in the vitally poorest human beings. Man's life is most open to disease. For in man's life, more than in any other being, there are divergent trends that must continuously be kept in unity. Health is not the lack of divergent trends in our bodily or mental or spiritual life, but the power to keep them united. And healing is the act of reuniting them after the disruption of their unity. 'Heal the sick' means – help them to regain their lost unity without depriving them of their abundance, without throwing them into a poverty of life, perhaps by their own consent.

For there is a sick desire to escape sickness by cutting off what can produce sickness. I have known people who are sick only because of their fear of sickness. Sometimes it may be necessary to reduce the richness of life, and to establish a poorer life on a smaller basis. But this in itself is not health. It is the most widespread mental disease. It can be transformed into health only if what is lost on a lower level is regained on a higher level, perhaps on the highest level – that of our infinite concern, our life with God.

Reduction to poverty of life is not healing. But where there is abundance there is also the danger of conflict, of disease and demonic bondage. In the light of this insight, let us look at a most important example, most important certainly for you who are sent to heal and to cast out demons – the Church that sends you. It may well be that the disease of many churches, denominations and congregations is that they try to escape disease by cutting off what can produce disease, and what also can produce greatness of life. A church that has ceased to risk sickness and even demonic influences has little power to heal and to cast out demons. Every minister who is proud of a smooth-running or gradually growing church should ask himself whether or not such a church is able to make its members aware of their sickness, and to give them the courage to accept the fact that they are healed. He should ask himself why the great creativity in all realms of man's spiritual life keeps itself consistently outside the churches. In many expressions of our secular culture, especially in the present decades, the awareness of man's sickness is great. Is it only because of prejudice that these people, who powerfully express the demonic bondage of man, do not look to the Church or to you, the ministers, for healing and for casting out demons? Or is it because of the lack of healing power in the Church, sick in its fear of sickness?

When Jesus asks the disciples to heal and to cast out demons, he does not distinguish between bodily and mental or spiritual diseases. But every page of the gospels demonstrates that he means all of them, and many stories show that he sees their inter-relationship, their unity. We see this unity today more clearly than many generations just behind us. This is a great gift, and you who have studied in the places you now are leaving have had much occasion to share in this gift. Above all, you have learned the truth of the good news – that laws and commands do not heal, but increase, the sickness of the sick. You have learned that the name of the healing power is grace, be it the grace of nature on which every physician depends, as even ancient medicine knew, or the grace in history that sustains the life of mankind by traditions and heritage and common symbols, or the grace of revelation that conquers the power of the demons by the message of forgiveness and of a new reality. And you have learned that disease that seems bodily may be mental at root, and that a disease that seems individual may be social at the same time, and that you cannot heal individuals without liberating them from the social demons that have contributed to their sickness. Beyond this, you may have become aware of the fact that both physical and mental, individual and social, illness is a consequence of the estrangement of man's spirit from the divine Spirit, and that no sickness can be healed nor any demon cast out without the reunion of the human spirit with the divine Spirit. For this reason you have become ministers of the message of healing. You are not supposed to be physicians; you are not supposed to be psychotherapists; you are not supposed to become political reformers. But you are supposed to pronounce and to represent the healing and demon-conquering power implied in the message of the Christ, the message of forgiveness and of a new reality. You must be conscious of the other ways of healing. You must co-operate with them, but you must not substitute them for what you represent.

Can you represent the Christian message? This may be your anxious question in this solemn hour. Should you ask me – can we heal without being healed ourselves? – I would answer – you can! For neither the disciples nor you could ever say – we are healed, so let us heal others. He who would believe this of himself is least fit to heal others; for he would be separating himself from them. Show them whom you counsel that their predicament is also your predicament.

And should you ask me – can we cast out demons without being liberated from demonic power ourselves? – I would answer – you can! Unless you are aware of the demonic possibility in yourselves, you cannot recognize the demon in others, and cannot do battle against it by knowing its name and thus depriving it of its power. And there will be no period in your life, so long as it remains creative and has healing power, in which demons will not split your souls and produce doubts about your faith, your vocation, your whole being. If they fail to succeed, they may accomplish something else – self-assurance and pride with respect to your power to heal and to cast out demons. Against this pride Jesus warns – 'Do not rejoice in this that the spirits are subject to you; but rejoice that your names are written in heaven.' And 'written in heaven' means written in spite of what is written against you in the records of your life.

Let me close with a word of reassurance. There is no greater vocation on earth than to be called to heal and to cast out demons. Be joyous in this vocation! Do not be depressed by its burden, nor even by the burden of having to deal with those who do not want to be healed. Rejoice in your calling. In spite of your own sickness, in spite of the demons working within you and your churches, you have a glimpse of what can heal ultimately, of him in whom God made manifest his power over demons and disease, of him who represents the healing power that is in the world, and sustains the world and lifts it up to God. Rejoice that you are his messengers. Take with you this joy when you leave this place!

6

Man and Earth

When I look at thy heavens, the work of thy fingers, the moon and the stars which thou hast established; what is man that thou art mindful of him, and the son of man that thou dost care for him? Yet thou hast made him little less than God, and dost crown him with glory and honour. Thou hast given him dominion over the works of thy hands; thou hast put all things under his feet.

PS. 8.3–6

I

Some time ago representatives of the world of science demanded a new line of research. They called it a 'science of survival'. They did not mean the survival of individuals or social groups, of nations or of races – that would not be new – but the survival of civilized mankind, or of mankind as a whole, or even of life altogether on the surface of this planet. Such a proposition is a sign that we have reached a stage of human history that has only one analogy in the past, the story of the 'Great Flood', found in the Old Testament and also among the myths and legends of many nations. The only difference between our situation and that of the Flood is that in these stories the gods or God bring about the destruction of life on earth because men have aroused divine anger. As the book of Genesis describes it: 'The Lord was sorry that he had made man on the earth and it grieved him to his heart. So the Lord said, I will blot out man, whom I have created, from the face of the ground, man and beast and creeping things and birds of the air, for I am sorry that I have made them.' In the next verse, the story answers the question of possible survival: 'But Noah found favour in the eyes of the Lord'. Through him, we read, not only man but also a pair of each species of animal was to make possible the survival of life upon the earth. Today, the destruction and survival of life have been given into the hands of man. Man who has dominion over all things, according to the psalm, has the power to save or destroy them, for he is little less than God.

How does man react to this new situation? How do *we* react? How *should* we react? 'The earth and we' has ceased to be merely a subject for human curiosity, artistic imagination, scientific study, or technical conquest. It has become a question of profound human concern and tormenting anxiety. We make desperate attempts to escape its seriousness. But when we look deep into the minds of our contemporaries, especially those of the younger generation, we discover a dread that permeates their whole being. This dread was absent a few decades ago and is hard to describe. It is the sense of living under a continuous threat; and although it may have many causes, the greatest of these is the imminent danger of a universal and total catastrophe. Their reaction to this feeling is marked either by a passionate longing for security in daily life, or an exaggerated show of boldness and confidence in man, based on his conquest of earthly and trans-earthly space. Most of us experience some of these contradictory reactions in ourselves. Our former naïve trust in the 'motherly' earth and her protective and preserving power has disappeared. It is possible that the earth may bear us no longer. We ourselves may prevent her from doing so. No heavenly sign, like the rainbow given to Noah as a promise that there would not be a second flood, has been given to us. We have no guarantee against man-made floods, that destroy not by water but by fire and air.

Such thoughts give rise to the question – what has the Christian message to say about this, our present predicament? What has it to say about life on this planet, its beginning and end, and man's place on it? What has it to say about the significance of the earth, the scene of human history, in view of the vastnesses of the universe? What about the short span of time allotted to this planet and the life upon it, as compared to the unimaginable length of the rhythms of the universe?

Such questions have been rarely asked in Christian teaching and preaching. For the central themes of Christianity have been the dramas of the creation and fall, of salvation and fulfilment. But sometimes peripheral questions move suddenly into the centre of a system of thought, not for any theoretical reason, but because such questions have become, for many, matters of life and death. This kind of movement has very often occurred in human history as well as in Christian history. And whenever it has occurred; it has changed man's view of himself in all respects, as it has changed the understanding of the Christian tradition on all levels. It may well be that we are living in such a moment, and that man's relation to the earth and the universe will, for a long time, become the point of primary concern for sensitive and thoughtful people. Should this be the case, Christianity certainly cannot withdraw into the deceptive security of its earlier questions and answers. It will be compelled forward into the more daring inroads of the human spirit, risking new and unanswered questions, like those we have just asked, but at the same time pointing in the direction of the eternal, the source and goal of man and his world.

Our predicament has been brought about chiefly by the scientific and technical development of our century. It is as foolish as it is futile to complain of this development. For there it lies before us – a realm created by man quite beyond the realm that was given him by nature when he first emerged from earlier forms of life. There it *is*, changing our lives and thoughts and feelings in all dimensions, consciously and, even more, unconsciously. Today's students are not what students of the preceding generation were. Today's hopes and anxieties are strange and often unintelligible to the older among us. And if we compare our two generations with any in earlier centuries, the distance separating us from them becomes really immense.

Since this sudden thrust forward has been brought about by science and its application, must not science itself have the last word about man, his earth and the universe? What can religion add? Indeed, has not religion, whenever it did try to explore these subjects, interfered with scientific development, and therefore been pushed aside? This certainly happened in the past, and is happening again today. But it is not religion in itself that interferes; it is the anxiety and fanaticism of religious people – laymen as well as theologians – marked by a flight from serious thought and an unwillingness to distinguish the figurative language of religion from the abstract concepts of scholarly research. In many sections of the Christian world, however, such distortion and misuse of religion have been overcome. Here one can speak freely of man and his earth in the name of religion, with no intention of adding anything to scientific and historical knowledge, or of prohibiting any scientific hypothesis, however bold.

What then has the Christian message to say about man's predicament in this world? The eighth Psalm, written hundreds of years before the beginning of the Christian era, raises the same question with full clarity and great beauty. It points, on the one hand, to the infinite smallness of man as compared to the universe of heavens and stars, and, on the other hand, to the astonishing greatness of man, his glory and honour, his power over all created things, and his likeness to God himself. Such thoughts are not frequent in the Bible. But when we come across them, they sound as though they had been written today. Ever since the opening of the universe by modern science, and the reduction of the great earth to a small planet in an ocean of heavenly bodies, man has felt real vertigo in relation to infinite space. He has felt as though he had been pushed out of the centre of the universe into an insignificant corner in it, and has asked anxiously – what about the high destiny claimed by man in past ages? What about the idea that the divine image is impressed in his nature? What about his history that Christianity always considered to be the point at which salvation for all beings took place? What about the Christ who, in the New Testament, is called the Lord of the universe? What about the end of history, described in biblical language as a cosmic catastrophe, in which the sun, the moon and the stars are perhaps soon to fall down upon the earth? What remains, in our present view of reality, of the importance of the earth and the glory of man? Further, since it seems possible that other beings exist on other heavenly bodies, in whom the divine image is also manifest, and of whom God is mindful, and also whom he has crowned with glory and honour, what is the meaning of the Christian view of human history and its centre, the appearance of the Christ?

These questions are not merely theoretical. They are crucial to every man's understanding of himself as a human-being placed upon this star, in an unimaginably vast universe of stars. And they are disturbing not only to people who feel grasped by the Christian message, but also to those who reject it but who share with Christianity a belief in the meaning of history and the ultimate significance of human life.

Again, the eighth Psalm speaks as though it had been conceived today – 'Thou hast made him little less than God; thou hast given him dominion over the works of thy hands'. It gives, as an example, man's dominion over the animals; but only since modern technology subjected all the spheres of nature to man's control has the phrase 'little less than God' revealed its full meaning. The conquest of time and space has loosened the ties that kept man in bondage to his finitude. What was once imagined as a prerogative of the gods has become a reality of daily life, accessible to human technical power. No wonder that we of today feel with the psalmist that man is little less than God, and that some of us feel even equal with God, and further that others would not hesitate to state publicly that mankind, as a collective mind, has replaced God.

We therefore have to deal with an astonishing fact: the same events that pushed man from his place in the centre of the world, and reduced him to insignificance, also elevated him to a God-like position both on earth and beyond!

Is there an answer to this contradiction? Listen to the psalmist: he does not say that man *has* dominion over all things or that man *is* little less than God; he says – '*Thou* hast given him dominion over the works of thy hands; *thou* hast made him little less than God'. This means that neither man's smallness nor his greatness emanates from himself, but that there is something above this contrast. Man, together with all things, comes from him who has put all things under man's feet. Man is rooted in the same Ground in which the universe with all its galaxies is rooted. It is this Ground that gives greatness to everything, however small it may be, to atoms as well as plants and animals; and it is this that makes all things small, however great – the stars as well as man. It gives significance to the apparently insignificant. It gives significance to each individual man, and to mankind as a whole. This answer quiets our anxiety about our smallness, and it quells the pride of our greatness. It is not a biblical answer only, nor Christian only, nor only religious. Its truth is felt by all of us, as we become conscious of our predicament – namely, that we are not of ourselves, that our presence upon the earth is not of our own doing. We are brought into existence and formed by the same power that bears up the universe and the earth and everything upon it, a power compared to which we are infinitely small, but also one which, because we are conscious of it, makes us great among creatures.

II

Now let us recall the words of God in the story of the Flood: 'I am sorry that I have made man'. They introduce a new element into our thinking about man and the earth – an element of judgment, frustration and tragedy. There is no theme in biblical literature, nor in any other, more persistently pursued than this one. The earth has been cursed by man innumerable times, because she produced him, together with all life and its misery, which includes the tragedy of human history. This accusation of the earth sounds through our whole contemporary culture, and understandably so. We accuse her in all our artistic expressions, in novels and drama, in painting and music, in philosophical thought and descriptions of human nature. But even more important is the silent accusation implied in our cynical denunciation of those who would say 'yes' to life, in our withdrawal from it into the refuges of mental disturbance and disease, in our forcing of life beyond itself or below itself by drugs and the various methods of intoxication, or in the social drugs of banality and conformity. In all these ways we accuse the destiny that placed us in this universe and upon this planet. 'Thou dost crown him with glory and honour', says the psalmist. But many of us long to get rid of that glory and wish we had never possessed it. We yearn to return to the state of creatures, which are unaware of themselves and their world, limited to the satisfaction of their animal needs.

In the story of the Flood it is God who is sorry that he made man, and who decides to blot him from the face of the earth. Today it is man who has the power to blot himself out, and often he is so sorry that he has been made man that he desires to withdraw from his humanity altogether. Many more people than we are aware of in our daily experience feel this desire; and perhaps something in us responds to them. Can it be that the earth, fully conquered by man, will cease to be a place where man wants to live? Is our passionate thrust into outer space perhaps an unconscious expression of man's flight from the earth? There are no sure answers to these questions, which, nevertheless, must be asked, because they cut through false feelings of security about the relation of man to the earth. The old insight that 'man is but a pilgrim on earth' is echoed in these questions, and applicable today to mankind as a whole. Mankind itself is a pilgrim on earth, and there will be a moment when this pilgrimage comes to an end, at some indefinitely remote time, or perhaps soon, in the very near future. Christianity gives no indication of the length of man's history; the early Church expected the end at any moment, and when it did not come and the Christians were profoundly disappointed, the span was extended. In modern times, the span has been stretched to an unlimited extent. Scientists speak today of the millions of years that human history could continue. Millions of years, or thousands of years, or tomorrow – we do not know! But we ask – what is the meaning of this history, whenever it began, whenever it will end? And we ask at the moment not what it means for you and me, but rather, what it means for the universe and its ultimate goal.

In the old story, God repented of having created man. The implication is that God took a risk when he created man, and every risk carries with it the possibility of failure. God himself considered the creation of man a failure, and made a new effort. But nothing assures us that this new effort did not also result in failure. The first time, according to the story, nature executed the divine judgment on man. This time, man may himself be the executioner. Should this occur, the privileged position of the earth, of which the astronomers speak and in which man has always believed, would seem to prove to have been of no avail. It would seem as though its unique role had been given it in vain.

We should not crowd such thoughts away, for they deserve to be taken seriously. Indeed, it seems to me, it is impossible for thoughtful people today to crowd them away. What has the Christian message to say about them? I repeat – it tells us nothing about the duration of human history. It does not say that it will continue after tomorrow, nor how it will come to an end in scientific terms. None of this is its concern. What the Christian message does tell us is that the meaning of history lies above history, and that, therefore, its length is irrelevant to its ultimate meaning. But it is not irrelevant with respect to the innumerable opportunities time affords for creation of life and spirit, and it is for these that we must fight with all our strength. Furthermore, if history should end tomorrow, through mankind's self-annihilation, the appearance of this planet and of man upon it will *not* have been in vain. For a being will have at least appeared once, in the billions of years of the universe, towards whose creation all the forces of life on earth worked together, and in whom the image of the divine Ground of all life was present. At least once, a living being will have come into existence, in whom life achieved its highest possibility – spirit. This is the ultimate source of man's greatness, and those of us who openly or covertly accuse life should open ourselves to this truth: in the short span of our life, and the short span of human history and even of the existence of this planet, something of eternal significance *did* happen – the depth of all things became manifest in *one* being, and the name of that being is *man*, and you and I are men! If we cannot accept this, and insist that this could have been so but was not, and that mankind is evil, and that the earth is contaminated by man's guilt, and that the blood of the murdered in all periods cries for revenge to heaven so that even God was forced to repent of his creation, then let us contemplate these words: 'The man Noah found favour in the eyes of God.' This one man represents something in every man that makes him a mirror of the divine in spite of evil and distortion. And the Christian message continues: there is one man in whom God found his image undistorted, and who stands for all mankind – the one, who for this reason, is called the Son and the Christ. The earth, contaminated by man, is purified and consecrated through man – namely, through the divine power of healing and fulfilment, of love and blessedness, made manifest in the one man and at work in all mankind, in all periods and in all places. This is what justifies human history, as it also justifies the earth that, for millions of years, prepared for the advent of man, and justifies the universe that produced the earth.

And yet, the universe is justified not only by the earth, nor is creation justified by man alone. Other heavenly bodies, other histories, other creatures in whom the mystery of being is manifest may replace us. Our ignorance and our prejudice should not inhibit our thought from transcending the earth and our history and even our Christianity. Science and the poetic imagination have made this leap, and Christianity should not hesitate to join them. Further, it should not hesitate to show that the Christian experience of divine power and glory implies an inexhaustible divine creativity, beyond the limits of earth or man and any part or state of the universe.

This means that we cannot seek for a beginning or an end of the universe within the past and future of measurable time. 'Beginning' and 'end' are not behind and before us, but above us in the eternal. From the eternal everything comes and to it everything goes, in every moment of life and history, in every moment of our planet and the universe to which it belongs. Creation is past *and* present. Fulfilment is future *and* present. It is in the present that past and future meet, because they come from, and go to, eternity.

The question of man and his earth, this question that has plunged our time into such anxiety and conflict of feeling and thought, cannot be answered without an awareness of the eternal presence. For only the eternal can deliver us from our sensation of being lost in the face of the time and space of the universe. Only the eternal can save us from the anxiety of being a meaningless bit of matter in a meaningless vortex of atoms and electrons. Only the eternal can give us the certainty that the earth, and with it, mankind, has not existed in vain, even should history come to an end tomorrow. For the last end is where the first beginning is, in him to whom 'a thousand years are but as yesterday'.

II

The Divine Reality

7

Spiritual Presence

Not that we are sufficient of ourselves to claim anything as coming from us; our sufficiency is from God, who has qualified us to be ministers of a new covenant, not in a written code but in the Spirit; for the written code kills, but the Spirit gives life.

II COR. 3.5–6

I

'Not that we are sufficient' – writes Paul. Who are 'we'? Obviously, 'we' are the apostle himself and those who work with him. These include all those who are qualified to serve the 'new covenant', as he calls it – namely, the new relationship between God and man, and through it the 'new creation', the new state of things in man and his world, of which Paul is a messenger. And everyone who participates in it, however fragmentarily, is qualified to serve. But when we ask, who *does* participate in the new creation, we soon find this to be an unanswerable question. For nobody can look into the innermost centre of another being, nor even fully into his own heart. Therefore, nobody can say with certainty that anyone else shares in the new state of things, and he can scarcely say it of himself. But even less can he say of another, however distorted the man's life may be, that he does not participate at all in the new reality, and that he is not qualified to serve its cause. Certainly, nobody can say this of himself.

Perhaps it is more important in our time to emphasize this last – namely, the qualification of ourselves and those around us to serve the new creation, our ability to be priests in mutual help towards achieving it. Not long ago, many people, especially members of the

Church, felt qualified to judge others and to tell them what to believe and how to act. Today we feel deeply the arrogance of this attitude. Instead, there is a general awareness of our lack of qualification, especially among the middle-aged and younger generations. We are inclined to disqualify ourselves, and to withdraw from the service of the new creation. We feel that we do not participate in it, and that we cannot bring others into such participation. We decline the honour and the burden of mutual priesthood. Often this is caused by unconcern for our highest human vocation. But it is equally caused by despair about ourselves, by doubt, guilt and emptiness. We feel infinitely removed from a new state of things, and totally unable to help others towards it.

But then the other words of our text must become effective, that our qualification is from God and not from ourselves, and the all-consoling word that God is greater than our heart. If we look beyond ourselves at that which is greater than we, then we can feel called to help others in just the moment when we ourselves need help most urgently – and astonishingly, we *can* help. A power works through us which is not of us. We may remember situations when words rose out of the depth of our being, perhaps in the midst of our own great anxiety, that struck another in the depth of *his* being and *his* great anxiety so strongly that they helped him to a new state of things. Perhaps we remember other situations when an action of a person, whose life we knew was disrupted, had a priestly awakening, and healing effect upon us. It did not come from him, but was in him, as it did not come from us, but was in us. Let us not assume the task of being mediators of the new creation to others arrogantly, be it in personal or ecclesiastical terms. Yet, let us not reject the task of being priest for each other because of despair about ourselves or unconcern about what should be our highest concern. Against both arrogance and despair stands the word that our qualification does not come from us, nor from any man or any institution, not even from the Church, but from God. And if it comes from God it is his spiritual presence in our spirit.

II

When we now hear the word 'Spirit', we are somehow prepared for it: the power in us, but not of us, qualifying us for the service of a new state of things is what Spirit means. This may sound strange to many both inside and outside the churches for whom the term Holy Spirit is the strangest of the strange terms that appear among Christian symbols. Rarely a subject of preaching, it is also neglected in religious teaching. Its festival, Pentecost, has almost disappeared in the popular consciousness of this country. Some groups that claim spiritual experiences of a particular character are considered unhealthy, and often rightly so. Liturgically, the use of the term 'Holy Ghost' produces an impression of great remoteness from our way of speaking and thinking. But spiritual experience is a reality for everyone, as actual as the experience of being loved or the breathing of air. Therefore, we should not shy away from the word 'Spirit'. We should become fully aware of the Spiritual Presence, around us and in us, even though we realize how limited our experience of 'God present to our spirit' may be. For this is what Divine Spirit means: God present to our spirit. Spirit is not a mysterious substance; it is not a part of God. It is God himself; but not God as the creative ground of all things and not God directing history and manifesting himself in its central event, but God as present in communities and personalities, grasping them, inspiring them, and transforming them.

For Spirit is first of all power, the power that drives the human spirit above itself towards what it cannot attain by itself, the love that is greater than all other gifts, the truth in which the depth of being opens itself to us, the holy that is the manifestation of the presence of the ultimate.

You may say again – 'I do not know this power. I have never had such an experience. I am not religious or, at least, not Christian and certainly not a bearer of the Spirit. What I hear from you sounds like ecstasy; and I want to stay sober. It sounds like mystery, and I try to illuminate what is dark. It sounds like self-sacrifice and I want to fulfil my human possibilities.' To this I answer – Certainly, the Spiritual Power can thrust some people into an ecstasy that most of us have never experienced. It can drive some towards a kind of self-sacrifice of which most of us are not capable. It can inspire some to insights into the depth of being that remain unapproachable to most of us. But this does not justify our denial that the Spirit is also working in us. Without doubt, wherever it works, there is an element, possibly very small, of self-surrender, and an element, however weak, of ecstasy, and an element, perhaps fleeting, of awareness of the mystery of existence. Yet these small effects of the spiritual power are enough to prove its presence.

But there are other conscious and noticeable manifestations of the Spiritual Presence. Let me enumerate some of them, while you ask yourselves whether and to what degree they are of your own experience. The Spirit can work in you with a soft but insistent voice, telling you that your life is empty and meaningless, but that there are chances of a new life waiting before the door of your inner self to fill its void and to conquer its dullness. The Spirit can work in you, awakening the desire to strive towards the sublime against the profanity of the average day. The Spirit can give you the courage that says 'yes' to life in spite of the destructiveness you have experienced around you and within you. The Spirit can reveal to you that you have hurt somebody deeply, but it also can give you the right word that reunites him with you. The Spirit can make you love, with the divine love, someone you profoundly dislike or in whom you have no interest. The Spirit can conquer your sloth towards what you know is the aim of your life, and it can transform your moods of aggression and depression into stability and serenity.

The Spirit can liberate you from hidden enmity against those whom you love and from open vengefulness against those by whom you feel violated. The Spirit can give you the strength to throw off false anxieties and to take upon yourself the anxiety which belongs to life itself. The Spirit can awaken you to sudden insight into the way you must take your world, and it can open your eyes to a view of it that makes everything new. The Spirit can give you joy in the midst of ordinary routine as well as in the depth of sorrow.

The Spirit can create warmth in the coldness you feel within you and around you, and it can give you wisdom and strength where your human love towards a loved one has failed. The Spirit can throw you into a hell of despair about yourself and then give you the certainty that life has accepted you just when you felt totally rejected, and when you rejected yourself totally. The Spirit can give you the power of prayer, that nobody has except through the Spiritual Presence. For every prayer – with or without words – that reaches its aim, namely the reunion with the divine Ground of our being, is a work of the Spirit speaking in us and through us. Prayer is the spiritual longing of a finite being to return to its origin.

These are works of the Spirit, signs of the Spiritual Presence with us and in us. In view of these manifestations, who can assert that he is without Spirit? Who can say that he is in no way a bearer of the Spirit? He may be in a small way. But is there anybody among us who could say more than that about himself?

One can compare the Spiritual Presence with the air we breathe, surrounding us, nearest to us, and working life within us. This comparison has a deep justification: in most languages, the word 'spirit' means breath or wind. Sometimes the wind becomes storm, grand and devastating. Mostly it is moving air, always present, not always noticed. In the same way the Spirit is always present, a moving power, sometimes in stormy ecstasies of individuals and groups, but mostly quiet, entering our human spirit and keeping it alive; sometimes manifest in great moments of history or a personal life, but mostly working hiddenly through the media of our daily encounters with men and world; sometimes using its creation, the religious communities and their spiritual means, and often making itself felt in spheres far removed from what is usually called religious. Like the wind the Spirit blows where it wills! It is not subject to rule or limited by method. Its ways with men are not dependent on what men are and do. You cannot force the Spirit upon yourself, upon an individual, upon a group, or even upon a Christian church. Although he who is the foundation of the Church was himself of the Spirit, and although the Spirit as it was present in him is the greatest manifestation of Spiritual Presence, the Spirit is not bound to the Christian Church or any one of them. The Spirit is free to work in the spirits of men in every human situation, and it urges men to let him do so; God as Spirit is always present to the spirit of man.

But why does the psalmist pray – 'Take not thy Spirit from me!'?
And why do we speak today of the 'absent God', a term which plays
a role in literature and art, and most of all in the personal experience
of innumerable people? How can we unite the message of the Spiritual Presence with the experience of the absent God? Let me say
something about the 'absent God', by asking – what is the cause of
his absence? We may answer – our resistance, our indifference, our
lack of seriousness, our honest or dishonest questioning, our genuine
or cynical doubt. All these answers have some truth, but they are
not final. The final answer to the question as to who makes God
absent is God himself!

It is the work of the Spirit that removes God from our sight,
not only for some men, but sometimes for many in a particular
period. We live in an era in which the God we know is the absent
God. But in knowing God as the absent God, we *know* of him; we
feel his absence as the empty space that is left by something or
someone that once belonged to us and has now vanished from our
view. God is always infinitely near and infinitely far. We are fully
aware of him only if we experience both of these aspects. But sometimes, when our awareness of him has become shallow, habitual –
not warm and not cold – when he has become too familiar to be
exciting, too near to be felt in his infinite distance, then he becomes
the absent God. The Spirit has not ceased to be present. The
Spiritual Presence can never end. But the Spirit of God hides God
from our sight. No resistance against the Spirit, no indifference, no
doubt can drive the Spirit away. But the Spirit that always remains
present to us can hide itself, and this means that it can hide God.
Then the Spirit shows us nothing except the absent God, and the
empty space within us which is *his* space. The Spirit has shown to
our time and to innumerable people in our time the absent God
and the empty space that cries in us to be filled by him. And then
the absent one may return and take the space that belongs to him,
and the Spiritual Presence may break again into our consciousness,
awakening us to recognize what we are, shaking and transforming
us. This may happen like the coming of a storm, the storm of the
Spirit, stirring up the stagnant air of our spiritual life. The storm
will then recede; a new stagnancy may take place; and the awareness

of the present God may be replaced by the awareness of the empty space within us. Life in the Spirit is ebb and flow – and this means – whether we experience the present or the absent God – it is the work of the Spirit.

III

And now let me describe a sympton of the Spiritual Presence within us, the greatest of all, most powerfully expressed in Paul's words – 'Not in a written code, but in the Spirit; for the written code kills but the Spirit gives life.' The work of the Spiritual Presence in a man reaches its height when it liberates him from the yoke of the commandments to the freedom of the Spirit. This is like a release from the sentence of death to a new life. A tremendous experience lies behind such words, an experience in which we all can share, but one that is rare in its full depth, and is then a revolutionary power that, through men like Paul and Augustine and Luther, changes the spiritual world and, through it, the history of mankind. Can we, you and I, share in such an experience?

First, have we not all felt the deadening power of the written code, written not only in the ten commandments and their many interpretations in the Bible and history, but also with the authoritative pen of parents and society into the unconscious depths of our being, recognized by our conscience, judging us by what we do and, above all, by what we are? Nobody can flee from the voice of this written code, written internally as well as externally. And if we try to silence it, to close our ears against it, the Spirit itself frustrates these attempts, opening our ears to the cries of our true being, of that which we are and ought to be in the sight of eternity. We cannot escape this judgment against us. The Spirit itself, using the written code, makes this impossible. For the Spirit does not give life without having led us through the experience of death. And, certainly, the written code in its threatening majesty has the power to kill. It kills the joy of fulfilling our being by imposing upon us something we feel as hostile. It kills the freedom of answering creatively what we encounter in things and men by making us look at a table of laws. It kills our ability to listen to the calling of the moment, to the voiceless voice of others, and to the here and now. It kills our courage to act, through the scruples of our anxiety-driven conscience. And among those who take it most seriously, it kills faith and hope, and throws them into self-condemnation and despair.

There is no way out from the written code. The Spirit itself prevents us from becoming compromisers, half fulfilling, half defying the commandments. The Spirit itself calls us back when we try to escape into indifference, or lawlessness, or (most usually) average self-righteousness. But when the Spirit calls us back, it does so not in order to *hold* us within the written code, but in order to give us life.

How can we describe the life that the Spirit gives us? I could use many words, well known to everybody, spoken by Paul himself, and after him by the great preachers and teachers of the Church. I could say that the work of the Spirit, liberating us from the law, is freedom. Or I could say that its work is faith, or that its work is hope, and, above all, that the Spirit creates love, the love in which all laws are confirmed and fulfilled and at the same time overcome. But if I used such words, the shadow of the absent God would appear and make you and me aware that we cannot speak like this today. If we did, freedom would be distorted into wilfulness, faith into belief in the absurd, hope into unreal expectations, and love – the word I would like most to use for the creation of the Spirit – into sentimental feeling. The Spirit must give us new words, or revitalize old words to express true life. We must wait for them; we must pray for them; we cannot force them. But we know, in some moments of our lives, what life is. We know that it is great and holy, deep and abundant, ecstatic and sober, limited and distorted by time, fulfilled by eternity. And if the right words fail us in the absence of God, we may look without words at the image of him in whom the Spirit and the Life are manifest without limits.

8

The Divine Name

You shall not take the name of the Lord your God in vain; for the Lord will not hold him guiltless who takes his name in vain.

EXOD. 20.7

There must be something extraordinary about the name if the second commandment tries to protect it as the other commandments try to protect life, honour, property. Of course, God need not protect himself, but he does protect his name, and so seriously that he adds to this single commandment a special threat. This is done because, within the name, that which bears the name is present. In ancient times, one believed that one held in one's power the being whose hidden name one knew. One believed that the saviour-god conquered the demons by discovering the mystery of the power embodied in their names, just as we today try to find out the hidden names of the powers that disrupt our unconscious depths and drive us to mental disturbances. If we gain insight into their hidden striving, we break their power. Men have always tried to use the divine name in the same way, not in order to break its power, but to harness its power for their own uses. Calling on the name of God in prayer, for instance, can mean attempting to make God a tool for our purposes. A name is never an empty sound; it is a bearer of power; it gives Spiritual Presence to the unseen. This is the reason the divine name can be taken in vain, and why one may destroy oneself by taking it in vain. For the invocation of the holy does not leave us unaffected. If it does not heal us, it may disintegrate us. This is the seriousness of the use of the divine name. This is the danger of religion, and even of anti-religion. For in both the name of God is used as well as misused.

Let me speak to you today of the danger of the use of the word God, when it is both denied and affirmed, and of the sublime embarrassment that we feel when we say 'God'. We may distinguish three forms of such embarrassment: the embarrassment of tact, the embarrassment of doubt, and the embarrassment of awe.

I

Not long ago, an intellectual leader was reported as saying, 'I hope for the day when everyone can speak again of God without embarrassment.' These words, seriously meant, deserve thoughtful consideration, especially in view of the fact that the last fifteen years have brought to this country an immense increase in the willingness to use the name of God – an unquestionable and astonishing revival, if not of religion, certainly of religious awareness. Do we hope that this will lead us to a state in which the name of God will be used without sublime embarrassment, without the restriction imposed by the fact that in the divine name there is more present than the name? Is an unembarrassed use of the divine name desirable? Is unembarrassed religion desirable? Certainly not! For the Presence of the Divine in the name demands a shy and trembling heart.

Everyone at one time or another finds himself in a situation where he must decide whether he shall use or avoid the name of God, whether he shall talk with personal involvement about religious matters, either for or against them. Making such a decision is often difficult. We feel that we should remain silent in certain groups of people because it might be tactless to introduce the name of God, or even to talk about religion. But our attitude is not unambiguous. We believe we are being tactful, when actually we may be cowardly. And then sometimes we accuse ourselves of cowardice, although it is really tact that prevents us from speaking out. This happens not only to those who would speak out *for* God, but also to those who would speak out *against* God. Whether for or against him, his name is on our lips and we are embarrassed because we feel that more is at stake than social tact. So we keep silent, uncertain as to whether we are right or wrong. The situation itself is uncertain.

Perhaps we might isolate ourselves or seem ridiculous by even mentioning the divine name, affirming or denying it. But there might also be another present for whom the mention of the divine name would produce a first experience of the Spiritual Presence and a decisive moment in his life. And again, perhaps there may be someone for whom a tactless allusion to God would evoke a definite sense of repulsion against religion. He may now think that religion *as such* is an abuse of the name of God. No one can look into the hearts of others, even if he converses with them intimately. We must risk *now* to talk courageously and *now* to keep silent tactfully. But in no case should we be pushed into a direct affirmation or denial of God which lacks the tact that is born of awe. The sublime embarrassment about his real presence in and through his name should never leave us.

Many persons have felt the pain of this embarrassment when they have had to teach their children the divine name, and others have felt it perhaps when they tried to protect their children against a divine name that they considered an expression of dangerous superstitition. It seems natural to teach children about most objects in nature and history without embarrassment, and there are parents who think it is equally natural to teach them divine things. But I believe that many of us as parents in this situation feel a sublime embarrassment. We know as Jesus knew that children are more open to the divine Presence than adults. It may well be, however, that if we use the divine name easily, we may close this openness and leave our children insensitive to the depth and the mystery of what is present in the divine name. But if we try to withhold it from them, whether because we affirm or because we deny it, emptiness may take hold of their hearts, and they may accuse us later of having cut them off from the most important thing in life. A Spirit-inspired tact is necessary in order to find the right way between these dangers. No technical skill or psychological knowledge can replace the sublimely embarrassed mind of parents or teachers, and especially of teachers of religion.

There is a form of misuse of the name of God that offends those who hear it with a sensitive ear, just because it did not worry those who misused it without sensitivity. I speak now of a public use of the name of God which has little to do with God, but much to do with human purpose – good or bad. Those of us who are grasped by the mystery present in the name of God are often stung when this name is used in governmental and political speeches, in opening prayers for conferences and dinners, in secular and religious advertisements, and in international war propaganda. Often the frequent use of the name of God is praised, as this is an indication that we are a religious nation. And one boasts of this, comparing one's nation with others. Should this be condemned? It is hard *not* to do so, but neither is it easy. If the divine name is used publicly with full conviction, and therefore with embarrassment and spiritual tact, it may be used without offence, although this is hardly ever so. It is usually taken in vain when used for purposes that are not to the glory of his name.

II

There is another more basic cause for sublime embarrassment about using the divine name – the doubt about God himself. Such doubt is universally human, and God would not be God if we could possess him like any object of our familiar world, and verify his reality like any other reality under inquiry. Unless doubt is conquered, there is no faith. Faith must overcome something; it must leap over the ordinary processes that provide evidence, because its object lies above the whole realm where scientific verification is possible. Faith is the courage that conquers doubt, not by removing it, but by taking it as an element into itself. I am convinced that the element of doubt, conquered in faith, is never completely lacking in any serious affirmation of God. It is not always on the surface; but it always gnaws at the depth of our being. We may know people intimately who have a seemingly primitive unshaken faith, but it is not difficult to discover the underswell of doubt that in critical moments surges up to the surface. Religious leaders tell us both directly and indirectly of the struggle in their minds between faith and unfaith. From fanatics of faith we hear beneath their unquestioning affirmations of God the shrill sound of their repressed doubt. It is repressed, but not annihilated.

On the other hand, listening to the cynical denials of God that are an expression of the flight from a meaning of life, we hear the voice of a carefully covered despair, a despair that demonstrates not assurance but doubt about their negation. And in our encounter with those who assume scientific reasons to deny God, we find that they are certain of their denial only so long as they battle – and rightly so – against superstititious ideas of God. When, however, they ask the question of God who is really God – namely, the question of the meaning of life as a whole and their own life, including their scientific work, their self-assurance tumbles, for neither he who affirms nor he who denies God can be ultimately certain about his affirmation or his denial.

Doubt, and not certitude, is our human situation, whether we affirm or deny God. And perhaps the difference between them is not so great as one usually thinks. They are probably very similar in their mixture of faith and doubt. Therefore, the denial of God, if serious, should not shake us. What should trouble everyone who takes life seriously is the existence of indifference. For he who is indifferent, when hearing the name of God, and feels, at the same time, that the meaning of his life is being questioned, denies his true humanity.

It is doubt in the depth of faith that often produces sublime embarrassment. Such embarrassment can be an expression of conscious or unconscious honesty. Have we not felt how something in us sometimes makes us stop, perhaps only for one moment, when we want to say 'God'? This moment of hesitation may express a deep feeling for God. It says something about the power of the divine name, and it says something about him who hesitates to use it. Sometimes we hesitate to use the word 'God' even without words, when we are alone; we may hesitate to speak to God even privately and voicelessly, as in prayer. It may be that doubt prevents us from praying. And beyond this we may feel that the abyss between God and us makes the use of his name impossible for us; we do not dare to speak to him, because we feel him standing on the other side of the abyss from us. This can be a profound affirmation of him. The silent embarrassment of using the divine name can protect us against violating the divine mystery.

III

We have considered the silence of tact and the silence of honesty concerning the divine name. But behind them both lies something more fundamental, the silence of awe, that seems to prohibit the speaking of God altogether. But is this the last word demanded by the divine mystery? Must we spread silence around what concerns us more than anything else – the meaning of our existence? The answer is – no! For God himself has given mankind names for himself in those moments when he has broken into our finitude and made himself manifest. We can and must use these names. For silence has power only if it is the other side of speaking, and in this way becomes itself a kind of speaking. This necessity is both our justification and our being judged, when we gather together in the name of God. We are an assembly where we speak about God. We are a church. The church is the place where the mystery of the holy should be experienced with awe and sacred embarrassment. But is this our experience? Are our prayers, communal or personal, a use or a misuse of the divine name? Do we feel the sublime embarrassment that so many people outside the churches feel? Are we gripped by awe when, as ministers, we point to the Divine Presence in the sacraments? Or, as theological interpreters of the holy, are we too sure that we can really explain him to others? Is there enough sacred embarrassment in us when fluent biblical quotations or quick, mechanized words of prayer pour from our mouths? Do we preserve the respectful distance from the Holy-Itself, when we claim to have the truth about him, or to be at the place of his Presence or to be the administrators of his Power – the proprietors of the Christ? How much embarrassment, how much awe is alive in Sunday devotional services all over the world?

And now let me ask the Church and all its members, including you and myself, a bold question. Could it be that, in order to judge the misuse of his name within the Church, God reveals himself from time to time by creating silence about himself? Could it be that sometimes he prevents the use of his name in order to protect his name, that he witholds from a generation what was natural to previous generations – the use of the word God? Could it be that godlessness is not caused only by human resistance, but also by God's paradoxical action – using men and the forces by which they are driven to judge the assemblies that gather in his name and take his name in vain? Is the secular silence about God that we experience everywhere today perhaps God's way of forcing his Church back to a sacred embarrassment when speaking of him? It may be bold to ask such questions. Certainly there can be no answer, because we do not know the character of the divine providence. But even without an answer, the question itself should warn all those inside the Church to whom the use of his name comes too easily.

Let me close with a few words that are both personal and more than personal. While thinking about this sermon I tried to make it not only one about the divine name, but also about God himself. Such an attempt stands under the judgment of the very commandment I tried to interpret, for it was a refined way of taking the name of God in vain. We can speak only of the names through which he has made himself known to us. For he himself 'lives in unapproachable light, whom no man has ever seen nor can see'.

9

God's Pursuit of Man

Then all the disciples forsook him and fled.

MATT. 26.56

I

Listening one evening to Bach's 'Passion according to St Matthew', I was struck by the text and music of the line, 'Then all the disciples forsook him and fled'. It anticipates the words of Jesus on the Cross, 'My God, my God, why hast thou forsaken me?' He who is forsaken by all men feels forsaken by God. And, indeed, all men left him, and those who were nearest him fled farthest from him. Ordinarily, we are not aware of this fact. We are used to imagining the crucifixion in terms of those beautiful pictures where, along with his mother and other women, at least one disciple is present. The reality was different. They all fled, and some women dared to watch from afar. Only an unimaginable loneliness remained during the hours his life and his work were broken.

How shall we think about these disciples? Our first reaction is probably the question – how *could* they forsake him whom they had called the Messiah, the Christ, the bringer of the new age, whom they had followed after leaving behind everything for his sake? But this time, when I heard the words and tones of the music, I admired the disciples! For it is *they* to whom we owe the words of our text. They did not hide their flight; they simply stated it in one short sentence, a statement that judges them for all time. The gospel stories contain many judgments against the disciples. We read that they misunderstood Jesus continuously, as did his mother and brothers, and that, day by day, their misunderstanding intensified his suffering. We read that some of the most important among them demanded a place of exceptional glory and power in the world to come. We read that Jesus reproached them because their zeal made them fanatical against those who did not follow him. And we read that Jesus had to call Peter 'Satan', because Peter tried to dissuade him from going to Jerusalem to his death, and that Peter denied his discipleship in the hour of trial. These reports are astonishing. They show what Jesus did to the disciples. He taught them to accept judgment, and not to present themselves in a favourable light. Without the acceptance of such judgment, they could not have been his disciples. And if the disciples had suppressed the truth about their own profound weakness, our gospels would not be what they are. The glory of the Christ and the misery of his followers would not be so clearly manifest. And yet even in the same records, man's desire to cover up his own ugliness makes itself felt. Later traditions in the gospels try to smooth the hard and hurting edges of the original picture. Apparently, it was unbearable to established congregations that *all* the disciples fled, that none of them witnessed the crucifixion and the death of the master. They could not accept the fact that only far away in Galilee was their flight arrested by the appearance of him whom they deserted in his hour of agony and despair. So, it was stated that Jesus himself had told them to go to Galilee; their flight was not a real flight. And still later, it was said that they did not flee at all, but remained in Jerusalem. From earliest times, the Church could not stand this judgment against itself, its past and its present. It has tried to conceal what the disciples openly admitted – that we all forsook him and fled. But this is the truth about all men, including the followers of Jesus today.

II

The flight from God begins in the moment we feel his presence. This feeling is at work in the dark, half-conscious regions of our being, unrecognized, but effective; in the restlessness of the child's asking and seeking; of the adolescent's doubts and despairs; of the adult's desires and struggles. God is present, but not as God; he is present as the unknown force in us that makes us restless.

But in some moments he appears *as* God. The unknown force in us that caused our restlessness becomes manifest as the God in whose hands we are, who is our ultimate threat and our ultimate refuge. In such moments it is as though we were arrested in our hidden flight. But it is not an arrest by brute force, but one that has the character of a question. And we remain free to continue our flight. This is what happened to the disciples: they were powerfully arrested when Jesus first called them, but they remained free to flee again. And they did when the moment of trial arrived. And so it is with the Church and all its members. They are arrested in their hidden flight and brought into the conscious presence of God. But they remain free to flee again, not only as individual men, but also as bearers of the Church, carrying the Church itself on the road to Galilee, separating it as far away as possible from the point where the eternal breaks into the temporal. Man flees from God even in the Church, the place where we are supposed to be arrested by the presence of God. Even there we are in flight from him.

III

If the ultimate cuts into the life of a man, he tries to take cover in the preliminary. He runs for a safe place, fleeing from the attack of that which strikes him with unconditional seriousness. And there are many places that look as safe to us as Galilee looked to the fleeing disciples.

Perhaps the most effective refuge in our time from the threatening presence of God is the work we are doing. This was not always so. The attitude of ancient man towards work is well summed up in the curse God pronounced over Adam – 'In the sweat of your face you shall eat bread', and in the words of the 90th Psalm concerning the short years of our life – 'yet their span is but toil and trouble'. Later, physical labour with its toil and its drudgery was left to the slaves and serfs or uneducated classes. And it was distinguished from creative work that was based on leisure time and, hence, the privilege of the few. Medieval Christianity considered work a discipline, especially in the monastic life. But in our period of our history, work has become the dominating destiny of all men, if not in reality, at least by demand. It is everything – discipline, production, creation. The difference between labour and work is gone. The fact that it stands under a curse in the biblical view is forgotten. It has become a religion itself, the religion of modern industrial society. And it has all of us in its grip. Even if we were able to escape the punishment of starvation for not working, something within us would not permit an escape from the bondage to work. For most of us it is both a necessity and a compulsion. And as such, it has become the favoured way of the flight from God.

And nothing seems to be safer than this way. From it we get the satisfaction of having fulfilled our duty. We are praised by others and by ourselves for 'work well done!' We provide support for our family or care for its members. We overcome daily the dangers of leisure, boredom and disorder. We acquire a good conscience out of it and, as a cynical philosopher said, at the end of it, a good sleep. And if we do the kind of work that is called creative, an even higher satisfaction results – the joy of bringing something new into being. Should somebody protest that this is not his way of fleeing from God, we might ask him: Have you not sometimes drawn a balance sheet of your whole being, and upon honestly discovering many points on the negative side, then balanced the sheet by your *work* on the other? The Pharisee of today would boast before God not so much of his obedience to the law and of his religious exercises as of his hard work and his disciplined, successful life. And he would also find sinners with whom he could compare himself favourably.

IV

There is another way to flee from God – the way that promises to lead us into the abundance of life, a promise that is kept to a certain extent. It is not necessarily the way of the prodigal son in the parable of Jesus. It can be the acceptance of the fullness of life, opened to us by a searching mind and the driving power of love towards the greatness and beauty of creation. Such longing for life does not need to close our eyes to the tragedy within greatness, to the darkness within light, to the pain within pleasure, to the ugliness within beauty. More men and women should dare to experience the abundance of life. But this also can be a way of fleeing from God, like labour and work. In the ecstasy of living, the limits of the abundance of life are forgotten. I do not speak of the shallow methods of having a good time, of the desire for fun and entertainment. This is, in most cases, the other side of the flight from God under the cover of labour and work, called recreation; it is justified by everybody as a means for working more effectively. But I speak of the ecstasy of living that includes participation in the highest and the lowest of life in one and the same experience. This demands courage and passion, but it also can be a flight from God. And whoever lives in this way should not be judged morally, but should be made aware of his restlessness, and his fear of encountering God. The man who is under the bondage of work should not boast of being superior to him. But neither should *he* boast to those who are in the bondage of work.

v

There are many in our time who have experienced the limits of both ways, for whom successful work has become as meaningless as plunging into the abundance of life. I am speaking of the sceptics and cynics, of those in anxiety and despair, of those who for a moment in their lives have been stopped in their flight from God and then continued it – though in a new form, in the form of consciously questioning or denying him. Their attitude is intensely described and analysed in our period by literature and the arts. And somehow they are justified. If they are serious sceptics, their seriousness, and the suffering following it, justifies them. If they are in despair, the hell of their serious despair makes them symbols through which we can better understand our own situation.

But they are also in flight from God. God has struck them; but they do not recognize him. Their need to deny him in thought and attitude shows that they have been arrested in their flight for a moment. If they were satisfied with the success of work or with the abundance of life, they would not have become 'accusers of being'. They accuse being, because they flee from the power that gives being to every being.

VI

This cannot be said of the last group of those who are in flight from God. They do not flee away from the Cross as did the disciples. They flee towards it. They watch it and witness to it; they are edified by it. They are better than the disciples! But are they really? If the Cross becomes a tenet of our religious heritage, of parental and denominational tradition, does it remain the Cross of Christ, the decisive point where the eternal cuts into the temporal? But perhaps it is not paternal tradition that keeps us near the Cross. Perhaps it is a sudden emotional experience, a conversion under the impact of a powerful preacher or evangelist that has brought us, for the first time, face to face with the Cross! Even then, in the height of our emotion, we should ask ourselves – is not our bow to the Cross the safest form of our flight from the Cross?

VII

But whatever the way of our flight from God, we can be arrested. And if this happens, something cuts into the regular processes of our life. It is a difficult but also great experience! One may be thrown out of work and think now that the meaning of life is gone. One may feel suddenly the emptiness of what seemed to be an abundant life. One may become aware that one's cynicism is not serious despair but hidden arrogance. One may see in the midst of a devotional act that one has exchanged God for one's religious feelings. All this is as painful as being wounded by a knife. But it is also great, because it opens up in us a new dimension of life. God has arrested us and something new takes hold of us.

This new reality that appears in us does not remove the old realities, but transforms them by giving them a new dimension. We still work; and work remains hard and full of anxiety and, as before, takes the largest part of our day! But it does not give us the meaning of our life. The strength or the opportunity to work may be taken from us, but not the meaning of our life. We realize that work cannot provide it and that work cannot take it from us. For the meaning of work itself has become something else. In working, we help to make real the infinite possibilities that lie hidden in life. We co-operate with life's self-creating powers, in the smallest or the greatest form of work. Through us, as workers, something of the inexhaustible depth of life becomes manifest. This is what one may feel, at least in some moments, if one is arrested by God. Work points beyond itself. And because it does so, it becomes blessed, and we become blessed through it. For blessedness means fulfilment in the ultimate dimension of our being.

And if someone is arrested by experiencing the profound emptiness of the abundant life, the abundance itself is not taken from him; it may still give great moments of ecstasy and joy. But it does not give him the meaning of his life. The external opportunities or the inner readiness to experience the ecstasies of life may vanish, but not the meaning of his life. He realizes that abundance cannot give it, and that want cannot take it away. For the abundance of life becomes something new for him who is arrested by God. It becomes a manifestation of the creative love that reunites what it separates, that gives and takes, that elevates us above ourselves and shows us that we are finite and must receive everything, that makes us love life and penetrate everything that is to its eternal ground.

And if someone is arrested by God and made aware of the lack of seriousness of his doubt and his despair, the doubt is not taken away from him, and the despair does not cease to be a threat. But his doubt does not have to lead to despair. It does not have to deprive him of the meaning of his life. Doubt cannot give it to him, as he secretly believed in his cynical arrogance; and doubt cannot take it from him, as he felt in his despair. For doubt becomes something else for him who is arrested by God. It becomes a means of penetrating the depth of his being and into the depth of all being.

Doubt ceases to be intellectual play or a method of research. It becomes a courageous undercutting of all the untested assumptions on which our lives are built. They break down one after the other, and we come deeper and nearer to the ground of our life. And then it happens that those who live in serious doubt about themselves and their world discover that dimension that leads to the ultimate by which they had been arrested. And they realize that hidden in the seriousness of their doubt was the truth.

And if someone is arrested by God and made aware of the ambiguous character of his religious life, religion is not taken away from him. But now he realizes that even this cannot give him the meaning of his life. He does not have to lose the meaning of his life if he loses his religion. Whoever is arrested by God stands beyond religion and non-religion. And if he holds fast to his religion, it becomes something else to him. It becomes a channel, not a law, another way in which the presence of the ultimate has arrested him, not the only way. Since he has reached freedom *from* religion, he also has reached freedom *for* religion. He is blessed in it and he is blessed outside of it. He has been opened to the ultimate dimension of being.

Therefore, don't flee! Let yourself be arrested and be blessed.

10

Salvation

Save us from the evil one.
MATT. 6.13

The last petition in our Lord's Prayer is known to all of us in the form: 'Deliver us from evil'. This form is not wrong, but it does not reach the depth of the original words which say: 'Save us from the evil one'. Let us meditate about them and, above all, about the one word 'save'.

Christianity has rightly been called a religion of salvation, and the 'Christ' is another word for him who brings salvation: the 'Saviour'. Salvation, saving, and saviour are words used many times in both the Old and the New Testament, innumerable times in the Church, in the works of the great theologians, in the hymns of the Christian poets, in liturgies and sermons, in solemn statements of the faith of the Church, in catechisms and, most important, in personal prayers. They permeate Christian thought and life as do few other words. How, then, is it possible to speak about them in the short space of a sermon?

Perhaps it is impossible! But even so, let me say with great seriousness that it is necessary, for the words which are most used in religion are also those whose genuine meaning is almost completely lost and whose impact on the human mind is nearly negligible. Such words must be reborn, if possible; and thrown away if this is not possible, even if they are protected by a long tradition. But there is only one way to re-establish their original meaning and power, namely, to ask ourselves what these words mean for our lives; to ask whether or not they are able to communicate something infinitely important to us. This is true of all important terms of our religious language: God and the Christ, the Spirit and the Church, sin and forgiveness, faith, love, and hope, Eternal Life, and the Kingdom of God. About each of them we must ask whether it is able to strike us in the depth of our being. If a word has lost this power for most of those in our time who are seriously concerned about things of ultimate significance, it should *not* be used again, or at least not as long as it is not reborn in its original power.

Perhaps it is still possible for the words salvation, saving, and saviour to be saved themselves. They are profound in their original meaning, but this has been covered by the dust of the centuries and emaciated by mechanical repetition. So let us try what may be impossible, and make 'salvation' the object of our thoughts in this hour.

The two translations of the seventh petition of our Lord's Prayer use two different images of what salvation is: 'saving' and 'delivering'. The word salvation is derived from the Latin word *salvus*, which means heal and whole. The saviour makes 'heal and whole' what is sick and disrupted. In Greece, the healing god, Asclepius, was called the saviour. Jesus calls himself the physician who has come to the sick and not to the healthy.

But saving also means delivering, liberating, setting free. This is another image: we are in bondage. It is the evil one – the symbol of the distorting and destroying powers in the world – that keeps us in servitude. The saviour, then, is the conqueror of the evil one and of his powers. No one has used this image more impressively than Paul in his great song of triumph in the eighth chapter of Romans, when he says that none of the demonic powers which govern this world can separate us from the love of God.

Saving is healing from sickness and saving is delivering from servitude; and the two are the same. Let me give you an example of their unity. We consider the neurotic or psychotic person who cannot face life as sick. But if we describe his disease, we find that he is under the power of compulsions from which he cannot extricate himself. He is, as the New Testament expresses it, demoniacally possessed. In him, disease and servitude are the same; and we ask whether, in some degree, this is not true of all of us. In which sense, we ask, do we need healing? in which sense liberation? What should salvation mean to us?

It is certainly not, what popular imagination has made of it, escaping from hell and being received in heaven, in what is badly called 'the life hereafter'. The New Testament speaks of eternal life, and eternal life is not continuation of life after death. Eternal life is beyond past, present, and future: we come from it, we live in its presence, we return to it. It is never absent – it is the divine life in which we are rooted and in which we are destined to participate in freedom – for God alone has eternity. Man should not boast of having an immortal soul as his possession for, as the letter to Timothy says: God 'alone has immortality'. We are mortal like every creature, mortal with our whole being – body and soul – but we are also kept in the eternal life *before* we lived on earth, *while* we are living in time, and *after* our time has come to an end.

If it is our destiny to participate in freedom in the divine life here and now, in and above time, we can say that the 'evil one' is he from whom we pray to be delivered: It is the enslaving power which prevents us from fulfilling our human destiny; it is the wall that separates us from the eternal life to which we belong; and it is the sickness of our being and that of our world caused by this separation. Salvation happens whenever the enslaving power is conquered, whenever the wall is broken through, whenever the sickness is healed. He who can do this is called the saviour. Nobody except God can do this. Those who are in chains cannot liberate themselves, and those who are sick cannot heal themselves. All liberating, all healing power comes from the other side of the wall which separates us from eternal life. Whenever it appears, it is a manifestation of eternal, divine life in our temporal and mortal existence. All liberators, all healers are sent by God; they liberate and heal through the power of the eternal given to them.

Who are these healers? Where are these saviours? The first answer is: They are *here*; they are *you*. Each of you has liberating and healing power over someone to whom you are a priest. We all are called to be priests to each other; and if priests, also physicians. And if physicians, also counsellors. And if counsellors, also liberators. There are innumerable degrees and kinds of saving grace. There are many people whom the evil one has enslaved so mightily that the saving power which may work through them has almost disappeared. On the other hand, there are the great saviour figures in whom large parts of mankind have experienced a lasting power of liberating and healing from generation to generation. Most of us are in between. And there is the one saviour in whom Christianity sees the saving grace without limits, the decisive victory over the demonic powers, the tearing down of the wall of guilt which separates us from the eternal, the healer who brings to light a new reality in man and his world. But if we call him the saviour we must remember that *God* is the saviour *through* him and that there are a host of liberators and healers, including ourselves, through whom the divine salvation works in all mankind. God does not leave the world at any place, in any time, without saviours – without healing power.

But now I must repeat a question asked before. What does all this mean for our own lives? When and where do we, ourselves, experience such saving power? When and where are we liberated, healed?

It is one of the most memorable facts in the biblical stories about Jesus that a large part of them are healing stories. There are three types: those in which people sick of body are directly healed; those in which people sick of body are forgiven and healed; and those in which people sick of mind are delivered from what was called demonic possession. It is regrettable that most preaching emphasizes the miraculous character of these stories, often using a poor, superstitious notion of miracles instead of showing the profound insight they betray into disease, health, and healing – the inseparable unity of body and mind. They are stories of salvation, performed by him who was called the Saviour. In them, it is visible that saving is healing. If the Church had shown more understanding of this part of its message, the regrettable split between religion and medicine might never have happened. In both, the power of saving is at work. If we look at the miracles of medical and mental healing today, we must say that here the wall between eternal and perishable life is pierced at *one* point; that liberation from the evil one has happened in *one* dimension of our life; that a physician or mental helper becomes a saviour for someone. He functions, as every saviour does, as an instrument of the healing power given to nature as well as to man by the divine presence in time and space.

But there are also limits to this kind of healing and liberating. The people healed by Jesus became sick again and died. Those who were liberated from demonic compulsion might, as Jesus himself warned, relapse into more serious states of mental disease. It was a breakthrough of eternal life in one moment of time, as all our medical healing is.

Also, there is a second limit of the healing of body and mind: The attitude of him who is to be healed may prevent healing. Without the desire for delivery from the evil one there is no liberation; without longing for the healing power, no healing! The wall which separates us from eternal life is broken through only when we desire it, and even then only when we trust in the bearers of healing power. Trust in saviours does not mean what is called today faith-healing, which is at best psychic sanctification of oneself or someone else. But it means openness to liberation from evil, whenever we encounter the possibility of such liberation.

This openness is not always present. We may prefer disease to health, enslavement to liberty. There are many reasons for the desire not to be healed, not to be liberated. He who is weak can exercise a power over his environment, over his family and friends, which can destroy trust and love but which gives satisfaction to him who exercises this power through weakness. Many amongst us should ask ourselves whether it is not this that we unconsciously do toward husband or wife; toward children or parents; toward friends or groups. There are others who do not want liberation because it forces them to encounter reality as it is and to take upon themselves man's heaviest burden: that of making responsible decisions. This is especially true of those who are in bondage to mental disturbances. Certainly they suffer, as do those with bodily diseases, but the compensation of gaining power or escaping responsibility appears more important to them than the suffering. They cut themselves off from the saving power in reality. For them, this saving power would first of all mean opening themselves up to the desire for salvation of body or mind. But even Jesus could not do it with many – perhaps most – of his listeners. One could perhaps say that the first work of every healer and liberator is to break through the love of disease and enslavement in those whom he wants to save.

Now let us look at quite a different form of enslavement and liberation brought about by our finitude in this world. In contrast to much of what has been said and much of what I myself have said against technology, I want to speak *for* the saving power of the technical control of nature. This is a bold statement to make in a period when such control has reached a peak and, at the same time, its injurious and destructive aspects have become more manifest than ever. Every technical invention elevates man above his animal stage, liberating him from much drudgery, conquering the narrow limits of his movements in time and space, saving him from innumerable smaller and greater evils to which he is subject as a part of nature; for instance, unnecessary pain and unnecessary death. These technical innovations have a saving power, as countless people have learned who have been broken in body and mind by being suddenly deprived of them. We know the destructive possibilities in technology; we know that it can annihilate all life on earth and bring history to an end. We also know that it can keep man's spirit away from salvation in a deeper and more lasting sense. We know that it can transform man himself into a thing and a tool. Nevertheless, in the great feats of technical control we have a breakthrough of the eternal into the temporal; they cannot be ignored when we speak of saving power and salvation.

In the ancient world, great political leaders were called saviours. They liberated nations and groups within them from misery, enslavement, and war. This is another kind of healing, reminiscent of the words of the last book of the Bible, which says in poetic language that 'the leaves of the tree of life are for the healing of the nations'. How can nations be healed? One may say: They can be liberated from external conquerors or internal oppressors. But can they be healed? Can they be saved? The prophets give the answer: Nations are saved if there is a small minority, a group of people, who represent what the nation is called to be. They may be defeated, but their spirit will be a power of resistance against the evil spirits who are detrimental to the nation. The question of saving power in the nation is the question of whether there is a minority, even a small one, which is willing to resist the anxiety produced by propaganda, the conformity enforced by threat, the hatred stimulated by ignorance. The future of this country and its spiritual values is not dependent as much on atomic defence as on the influence such groups will have on the spirit in which the nation will think and act.

And this is true of mankind as a whole. Its future will be dependent on a saving group, embodied in one nation or crossing through all nations. There is saving power in mankind, but there is also the hidden will to self-destruction. It depends on every one of us which side will prevail. There is no divine promise that humanity will survive this or the next year. But it may depend on the saving power effective in you or me, whether it will survive. (It may depend on the amount of healing and liberating grace which works through any of us with respect to social justice, racial equality, and political wisdom.) Unless many of us say to ourselves: Through the saving power working in me, mankind may be saved or lost – it will be lost.

But in order to be the bearers of saving power, we must be saved ourselves; the wall separating us from eternal life must be broken through. And here is one thing which strengthens the wall and keeps us sick and enslaved. It is our estrangement and guilt which are the impediments which keep us from reaching eternal life here and now. The judgment against us which we confirm in our conscience is the sickness unto death, the despair of life, from which we must be halted in order to say *yes* to life. Healed life is new life, delivered from the bondage of the evil one. Here the last two petitions of our Lord's Prayer become one petition: forgive our trespasses, and deliver us from the evil one – this is one and the same thing. And if we call Jesus, the Christ, our saviour, then we mean that in him we see the power which heals us by accepting us and which liberates us by showing us in his being a new being – a being in which there is reconciliation with ourselves, with our world, and with the divine ground of our world and ourselves.

And now the last question: Who shall be saved, liberated, healed? The fourth gospel says: The world! The reunion with the eternal from which we come, from which we are separated, to which we shall return, is promised to everything that is. We are saved not as individuals, but in unity with all others and with the universe. Our own liberation does not leave the enslaved ones alone, our own healing is a part of the great healing of the world. Therefore, two other petitions of our Lord's Prayer also ask the same: Save us from the evil one, and thy Kingdom come! This Kingdom is his creation, liberated and healed. This is what we hope for when we look from time to eternity. Deliver us – heal us – that is the cry of everything that is; of each of us in unity with all mankind and in unity with the whole universe. The divine answer is: I shall return to me what is separated from me because it belongs to me. I am liberating you today as I did before and will do in the future. Today, when you hear these words, 'I am liberating you, I am healing you', do not resist!

11

The Eternal Now

I am the Alpha and the Omega, the beginning and the end.
REV. 21.6

It is our destiny and the destiny of everything in our world that we must come to an end. Every end that we experience in nature and mankind speaks to us with a loud voice: you also will come to an end! It may reveal itself in the farewell to a place where we have lived for a long time, the separation from the fellowship of intimate associates, the death of someone near to us. Or it may become apparent to us in the failure of a work that gave meaning to us, the end of a whole period of life, the approach of old age, or even in the melancholy side of nature visible in autumn. All this tells us: you will also come to an end.

Whenever we are shaken by this voice reminding us of our end, we ask anxiously – what does it mean that we have a beginning and an end, that we come from the darkness of the 'not yet' and rush ahead towards the darkness of the 'no more'? When Augustine asked this question, he began his attempt to answer it with a prayer. And it is right to do so, because praying means elevating oneself to the eternal. In fact, there is no other way of judging time than to see it in the light of the eternal. In order to judge something, one must be partly within it, partly out of it. If we were totally within time, we would not be able to elevate ourselves in prayer, meditation and thought, to the eternal. We would be children of time like all other creatures and could not ask the question of the meaning of time. But as men we are aware of the eternal to which we belong and from which we are estranged by the bondage of time.

I

We speak of time in three ways or modes – the past, present and future. Every child is aware of them, but no wise man has ever penetrated their mystery. We become aware of them when we hear a voice telling us: you also will come to an end. It is the future that awakens us to the mystery of time. Time runs from the beginning to the end, but our awareness of time goes in the opposite direction. It starts with the anxious anticipation of the end. In the light of the future we see the past and present. So let us first consider our going into the future and towards the end that is the last point that we can anticipate in our future.

The image of the future produces contrasting feelings in man. The expectation of the future gives one a feeling of joy. It is a great thing to have a future in which one can actualize one's possibilities, in which one can experience the abundance of life, in which one can create something new – be it new work, a new living being, a new way of life, or the regeneration of one's own being. Courageously one goes ahead towards the new, especially in the earlier part of one's life. But this feeling struggles with other ones: the anxiety about what is hidden in the future, the ambiguity of everything it will bring us, the shortness of its duration that decreases with every year of our life and becomes shorter the nearer we come to the unavoidable end. And finally the end itself, with its impenetrable darkness and the threat that one's whole existence in time will be judged as a failure.

How do men, how do *you*, react to this image of the future with its hope and threat and inescapable end? Probably most of us react by looking at the immediate future, anticipating it, working for it, hoping for it, being anxious about it, while cutting off from our awareness the future which is farther away, and above all, by cutting off from our consciousness the end, the last moment of our future. Perhaps we could not live without doing so most of our time. But perhaps we will not be able to die if we *always* do so. And if one is not able to die, is he really able to live?

How do we react if we become aware of the inescapable end

contained in our future? Are we able to bear it, to take its anxiety into a courage that faces ultimate darkness? Or are we thrown into utter hopelessness? Do we hope against hope, or do we repress our awareness of the end because we cannot stand it? Repressing the consciousness of our end expresses itself in several ways.

Many try to do so by putting the expectation of a long life between now and the end. For them it is decisive that the end be delayed. Even old people who are near the end do this, for they cannot endure the fact that the end will not be delayed much longer.

Many people realize this deception and hope for a continuation of this life after death. They expect an endless future in which they may achieve or possess what has been denied them in this life. This is a prevalent attitude about the future, and also a very simple one. It denies that there *is* an end. It refuses to accept that we are creatures, that we come from the eternal ground of time and return to the eternal ground of time and have received a limited span of time as *our* time. It replaces eternity by endless future.

But endless future is without a final aim; it repeats itself and could well be described as an image of hell. This is not the Christian way of dealing with the end. The Christian message says that the eternal stands above past and future. 'I am the Alpha and the Omega, the beginning and the end.'

The Christian message acknowledges that time runs towards an end, and that we move towards the end of that time which is our time. Many people – but not the Bible – speak loosely of the 'hereafter' or of the 'life after death'. Even in our liturgies eternity is translated by 'world without end'. But the world, by its very nature, is that which comes to an end. If we want to speak in truth without foolish, wishful thinking, we should speak about the eternal that is neither timelessness nor endless time. The mystery of the future is answered in the eternal of which we may speak in images taken from time. But if we forget that the images are images, we fall into absurdities and self-deceptions. There is not time *after* time, but there is eternity *above* time.

II

We go towards something that is not yet, and we come from something that is no more. We are what we are by what we came from. We have a beginning as we have an end. There was a time that was not *our* time. We hear of it from those who are older than we; we read about it in history books; we try to envision the unimaginable billions of years in which neither we nor anyone was who could tell us of them. It is hard for us to imagine our 'being-no-more'. It is equally difficult to imagine our 'being-not-yet'. But we usually don't care about our not yet being, about the indefinite time before our birth in which we were not. We think: *now* we are; this is *our* time – and we do not want to lose it. We are not concerned about what lies before our beginning. We ask about life after death, yet seldom do we ask about our being before birth. But is it possible to do one without the other? The fourth gospel does not think so. When it speaks of the eternity of the Christ, it does not only point to his return to eternity, but also this coming *from* eternity. 'Truly, truly, I say to you, before Abraham was, I *am*.' He comes from another dimension than that in which the past lies. Those to whom he speaks misunderstand him because they think of the historical past. They believe that he makes himself hundreds of years old and they rightly take offence at this absurdity. Yet he does not say, 'I *was*' before Abraham; but he says, 'I *am*' before Abraham was. He speaks of his beginning out of eternity. And this is the beginning of everything that is – not the uncounted billions of years but the eternal as the ultimate point in our past.

The mystery of the past from which we come is that it is and is not in every moment of our lives. It is, in so far as we are what the past has made of us. In every cell of our body, in every trait of our face, in every movement of our soul, our past is the present.

Few periods knew more about the continuous working of the past in the present than ours. We know about the influence of childhood experiences on our character. We know about the scars left by events in early years. We have rediscovered what the Greek tragedians and the Jewish prophets knew, that the past is present

in us, both as a curse and as a blessing. For 'past' always means
both a curse and a blessing, not only for individuals, but also for
nations and even continents.

History lives from the past, from its heritage. The glory of the
European nations is their long, inexhaustibly rich tradition. But the
blessings of this tradition are mixed with curses resulting from early
splits into separated nations whose bloody struggles have filled century
after century and brought Europe again and again to the edge of self-
destruction. Great are the blessings *this* nation has received in the
course of its short history. But from earliest days, elements have been
at work that have been and will remain a curse for many years to come.
I could refer, for instance, to racial consciousness, not only within the
nation itself, but also in its dealings with races and nations outside its
own boundaries. 'The American way of life' is a blessing that comes
from the past; but it is also a curse, threatening the future.

Is there a way of getting rid of such curses that threaten the life
of nations and continents and, more and more, of mankind as a
whole? Can we banish elements of our past into the past so that
they lose their power over the present? In man's individual life this
is certainly possible. One has rightly said that the strength of a
character is dependent on the amount of things that he has thrown
into the past. In spite of the power his past holds over him, a man
can separate himself from it, throw it out of the present into the
past in which it is condemned to remain ineffective – at least for a
time. It may return and conquer the present and destroy the person,
but this is not necessarily so. We are not inescapably victims of our
past. We can make the past remain nothing but *past*. The act in
which we do this has been called repentance. Genuine repentance
is not the feeling of sorrow about wrong actions, but it is the act of
the whole person in which he separates himself from elements of
his being, discarding them into the past as something that no longer
has any power over the present.

Can a nation do the same thing? Can a nation or any other social
group have genuine repentance? Can it separate itself from curses
of the past? On this possibility rests the hope of a nation. The
history of Israel and the history of the Church show that it is possible
and they also show that it is rare and extremely painful. Nobody

knows whether it will happen to *this* nation. But we know that its future depends on the way it will deal with its past, and whether it can discard into the past elements which are a curse!

In each human life a struggle is going on about the past. Blessings battle with curses. Often we do not recognize what are blessings and what are curses. Today, in the light of the discovery of our unconscious strivings, we are more inclined to see curses than blessings in our past. The remembrance of our parents, which in the Old Testament is so inseparably connected with their blessings, is now much more connected with the curse they have unconsciously and against their will brought upon us. Many of those who suffer under mental afflictions see their past, especially their childhood, only as the source of curses. We know how often this is true. But we should not forget that we would not be able to live and to face the future if there were not blessings that support us and which come from the same source as the curses. A pathetic struggle over their past is going on almost without interruption in many men and women in our time. No medical healing can solve *this* conflict, because no medical healing can change the past. Only a blessing that lives above the conflict of blessing and curse can heal. It is the blessing that changes what seems to be unchangeable – the past. It cannot change the facts; what has happened has happened and remains so in all eternity! But the *meaning* of the facts can be changed by the eternal, and the name of this change is the experience of 'forgiveness'. If the meaning of the past is changed by forgiveness, its influence on the future is also changed. The character of curse is taken away from it. It becomes a blessing by the transforming power of forgiveness.

There are not always blessings and curses in the past. There is also emptiness in it. We remember experiences that, at the time, were seemingly filled with an abundant content. Now we remember them, and their abundance has vanished, their ecstasy is gone, their fullness has turned into a void. Pleasures, successes, vanities have this character. We do not feel them as curses; we do not feel them as blessings. They have been swallowed by the past. They did not contribute to the eternal. Let us ask ourselves how little in our lives escapes this judgment.

The mystery of the future and the mystery of the past are united in the mystery of the present. Our time, the time we have, is the time in which we have 'presence'. But how can we have 'presence'? Is not the present moment gone when we think of it? Is not the present the ever-moving boundary line between past and future? But a moving boundary is not a place to stand upon. If nothing were given to us except the 'no more' of the past and the 'not yet' of the future, we would not have anything. We could not speak of the time that is *our* time; we would not have 'presence'.

The mystery is that we *have* a present; and, even more, that we have *our* future also because we anticipate it in the present; and that we have *our* past also, because we remember it in the present. In the present our future and our past are *ours*. But there is no 'present' if we think of the never-ending flux of time. The riddle of the present is the deepest of all the riddles of time. Again, there is no answer except from that which comprises all time and lies beyond it – the eternal. Whenever we say 'now' or 'today', we stop the flux of time for us. We accept the present and do not care that it is gone in the moment that we accept it. We live in it and it is renewed for us in every new 'present'. This is possible because every moment of time reaches into the eternal. It is the eternal that stops the flux of time for us. It is the eternal 'now' which provides for us a temporal 'now'. We live so long as 'it is still today' – in the words of the letter to the Hebrews. Not everybody, and nobody all the time, is aware of this 'eternal now' in the temporal 'now'. But sometimes it breaks powerfully into our consciousness and gives us the certainty of the eternal, of a dimension of time which cuts into time and gives us our time.

People who are never aware of this dimension lose the possibility of resting in the present. As the letter to the Hebrews describes it, they never enter into the divine rest. They are held by the past and cannot separate themselves from it, or they escape towards the future, unable to rest in the present. They have not entered the eternal rest which stops the flux of time and gives us the blessing of the present. Perhaps this is the most conspicuous characteristic of our period, especially in the western world and particularly in this country. It lacks the courage to accept 'presence' because it has lost the dimension of the eternal.

'I am the beginning and the end.' This is said to us who live in the bondage of time, who have to face the end, who cannot escape the past, who need a present to stand upon. Each of the modes of time has its peculiar mystery, each of them carries its peculiar anxiety. Each of them drives us to an ultimate question. There is *one* answer to these questions – the eternal. There is *one* power that surpasses the all-consuming power of time – the eternal: He who was and is and is to come, the beginning and the end. He gives us forgiveness for what has passed. He gives us courage for what is to come. He gives us rest in his eternal Presence.

III

The Challenge to Man

12

Do not be Conformed

Do not be conformed to this aeon, but be transformed by the renewal of your mind.

ROM. 12.2*a*

'Do not be conformed.' This warning of Paul is significant for all periods of history. It is urgently needed in our period. It applies to each of us, to our civilization, to mankind as a whole. It has many facets because of the many things to which one may be conformed. But there is *one* all-embracing thing to which the apostle does not want us to be conformed – this aeon. Instead of being conformed to this aeon he wants us to be transformed by the coming aeon, the state of renewal of our world and of ourselves. Not conformity, but transformation – that is what Paul says in the words of our text.

Our period has experienced many revolutionary transformations. The older ones amongst us remember them, often because they have suffered under them in their early lives. Today, both old and young are reacting against revolutions and further transformations of the world in which they have settled down. A mood of conservatism permeates large sections of mankind and certainly the people in our western civilization. This is natural and, as such, need not be a matter of concern. But it must become a matter of concern and be challenged if conservatism becomes conformism, if the motto of the new generation is – not transformation, but conformity. And this seems to be the case starting in school days, when some teachers prevent individual friendships because they threaten 'adjustments' (this fallacious principle of education), on through the years when the laws of the gang are more important for the youngster than all divine and human laws together; through the years in the institutes of higher learning where the standards imposed by older upon younger students allow the most extravagant behaviour; through the years of entrance into the world of adult competition and adaptation to the means of success; through the years of maturity and power and the fear of violating social, political and religious taboos and through the later years of one's life when religious propagandists use the fear of the approaching end to preach new forms of old religious conformisms. All these stages of our life are accompanied by incessant pressure from the communications media, one of whose functions is to produce conformity without letting people even become aware of it.

'Do not be conformed', says the apostle, challenging, in these four words, the main trend of our whole present civilization. But he challenges more than this. He challenges you and me, whether we are caught by this civilization or not. We may be conformist not only if we agree but also if we disagree, and we may be non-conformist, not only if we disagree but also if we agree. They are words of warning for those of us who believe that their revolutionary thrust liberates us from the danger of conformism. For it does not. The revolutionary gang can be as conformist as the conservative group.

One can be conformed not only to a group, but also to oneself. The revolutionary can become used to himself as a revolutionary, so that he loses his freedom and becomes a conformist to revolution. In the same way one can be conformed to one's attitude of indifference or to cynicism or strictness or perfectionism, or one's own emptiness. One can be conformed to oneself and be prevented from transforming oneself by a renewal of the spirit. One can be non-conformist without love, unable to transform anything because one has not transformed oneself.

Why does Paul attack conformism? Why does he not call the Christian the perfectly adjusted man? Why does he not describe the Christian way as the way to a complete acceptance of the moral and religious standards of society? His thought is far from this, and certainly he could not have been called a good educator according to the criterion of 'adjustment'. But he knew why he rejected conformism. He knew that all conformism is a state of being conformed to *this* aeon. So let us try to understand the meaning of this strange assertion. This aeon means the state of things in which we are living, which is, according to Paul, a state of corruption. Being conformed to it, therefore, means to participate in its corruptedness. Where there is conformism there is acceptance of corruption, subjection to the present questionable state of things. In our English Bibles, the Greek word for aeon is translated 'world'. This is somehow misleading. When we speak of world we think of the universe. But the universe, including our earth and everything in it, is the product of incessant divine creativity here and now. It is good in its created form, and it is the place to which the kingdom of God shall come, as we pray in the Lord's Prayer. It is one of the most dangerous misunderstandings of the Christian message to deny this world and its created glory, and to direct our eyes to a superworld, unrelated to the original creation. The Bible speaks of a new heaven and a new earth in contrast to the old heaven and the old earth. And now we understand what Paul means when he speaks of conformity to this aeon: he means the untransformed old earth and the untransformed old heaven. He means the corrupted state of the universe, and especially of our universe – the universe of men – when he warns us not to become conformed to it. The attitude towards this aeon, towards ourselves, and towards our world that the apostle demands is threefold: judgment, resistance, and transformation.

But one may ask – must I judge, must I resist, must I transform everything I encounter? Ought we not to adjust to that which is born out of the wisdom of the ages, bestowed upon us by the generations before us through their experience and insights? Could one not say – be conformed to what has been proved to be good and noble and in conformity with the spirit of love? We must ask this question with great seriousness and self-criticism. But we must not forget that we are living in *this* aeon, under the control of its forms and ways, where the uncorrupted is mixed with corruption, and the acceptable with the unacceptable, and good with evil. This is what makes conformity so dangerous. If the corruption of this aeon were obvious, very few would be tempted to be conformed to it. Not many people, in reality or in literature, make a pact with the devil. But there are many who are lured by elements of goodness, indeed of real goodness, into a pact with this aeon, into the state of being conformed to it. And, certainly, there are strong arguments for accepting conformity. We all are conformed to the family into which we are born whether we want to be or not. Shall we try to be non-conformists in our family because conformism would mean adjustment to this aeon, to the corrupted state of things? Would that not bring much suffering to the other members of the family, and deprive us of the many blessings that an intimate and ordered family life can provide? How can the commandment to honour father and mother be combined with the warning of the apostle not to be conformed to this aeon? Jesus says – 'I have come to set a man against his father and a daughter against her mother and a daughter-in-law against her mother-in-law; and a man's foes will be those of his own household. He who loves father or mother more than me is not worthy of me; and he who loves son or daughter more than me is not worthy of me' (Matt. 10.35–37). These are the most radical statements of non-conformity. And even Paul's radicalism sounds conservative in comparison with them. It is astonishing that a faith based on words like these has been used throughout its history as a most successful instrument of conformity inside and outside family relations. How did this happen? Why is it the predominant attitude within Western culture even today, in spite of all the forces of disintegration? It is infinitely difficult to find the point where the state of being conformed contradicts love as it is manifest in the Christ. It would be easy to notice the point where separation becomes unavoidable, if our family, as often was the case in early Christianity, tried to make us reject the Christ and what he stands for. But this is not so today. Instead of it, the question of conforming or not conforming arises in innumerable small moments of our daily life. And in each moment, our answer is a risk, burdened with struggles within our own conscience. We do not know with certainty whether our non-conformity is based on a wrong conformity to ourselves or whether it is our awareness of corruption that drives us to non-conformity. And we do not know with certainty whether our non-resistance is based on a wrong surrender or whether it is an element of love and wisdom that keeps us conformed to the family group. We do not know these things with certainty, and we can act only at the risk of being wrong. But act we must. Most people try to avoid the risk by being conformed to the state of things into which they have been thrown by destiny. But those who have transformed our world risked wrong decisions. And the greater men they were, the more conscious were they of the risk. They did not cease to doubt in spite of the depth and the passion of their faith. For when they refused to be conformed to their families and traditions, they were not instead conformed to themselves, but were renewed in their own being and could thus renew other beings. And precisely for this reason they never became self-assured – they took upon themselves the risk of not being conformed and the anxiety and doubt and glory of this risk.

Paul demands this of every Christian. Every Christian must be strong enough to risk non-conformity, even in the radical sense that Jesus describes with respect to one's family. The situation in the family is an example, and more than an example. For all conformity is rooted in it. And resistance to conformity is first of all resistance to the family. But there are other larger groups in which we breathe the air of conformity day and night, and where resistance is sometimes easier, yet often more difficult, than in the family. I am thinking of educational, social, political, and religious groups. Let us look at each of them in the light of the apostolic word.

It seems that an educational group is least exposed to conformity. Those who are learning are usually more inclined to resist than to accept their teachers and what they are taught by them. And the teachers are chosen on the basis of the independence of their judgments and the freedom of their scholarly questioning. This seems to make the institutions of higher learning the representative places of non-conformity. I do not think that this is so, however. One only needs to ask the students two questions: Don't you often build, out of your resistance to what you are taught, a new conformity of rebellion? And do you resist the group or gang to which you belong as strongly as you resist your teachers, or are you conquered by gang conformity and all the elements of this aeon, and the corruption implied in such conformity? How would you answer?

And one only needs to ask us teachers two questions: Are we

fully aware of our dependence on the intellectual fashion, especially when it receives social or political support? And have we perhaps become – and more so as we grow older – conformed to ourselves, to the fixed opinions on which we rest? I believe that all of us, both students and teachers, would fall silent if asked these questions. The institutions of higher learning have no monopoly of non-conformity. They need transformation as much as any other group. They also belong to *this* aeon.

Families and schools are part of those larger groups that we call society and state. Much has been said and written about the conformist influence that both of them exercise on the way of life of each of us. I do not need to repeat these often trenchant and distressing observations. I do not need to point to the pressures exerted by suburban neighbourhoods, by the laws of competition, by political threats, and by radio and TV, filling our air waves twenty-four hours daily and impressing our unconscious even as we try to resist them in our conscious centre. Again, the difficulty in resisting the conformist impact of all this is that it is not only evil but also good. This mixture of good and evil in our social and political forms makes every act of protest a risk, not in the sense that we risk friendship, acknowledgment, or success – this we might be able to do – but in the sense that we risk making the wrong decision and losing ourselves in it. But even so, we must risk, as the disciples to whom Jesus spoke had to risk. We must risk 'being delivered up to councils, to stand before governors and kings, to bear testimony before them, to be put to death by friends and relatives, to be hated by all'. This is certainly a picture of an extreme situation, although it has happened in our century to many people. Most of us will probably never have to face such grave decisions. But in our daily life, in dealing with society and state, we have to face social tribunals that accuse us and may condemn us, because we are not conformed to their way of life. The picture of extreme non-conformity that Jesus paints includes all the small acts of non-conformity that we must perform in our daily life. Do not be conformed to the society group to which you belong. Do not be conformed to those who have political power over you, even if you obey them. But work for their transformation.

Many churchmen would perhaps agree with this. But they would resist, if one applied the warning of the apostle to the Church itself. But we must do so. The conformism that threatened Jesus most effectively and brought him to death was the religious conformism of his time. And the situation was and is not different in the Church. For the Christian churches also belong to this aeon, although they witness to the coming aeon and represent the coming aeon in time and space. They share in the corruption of this aeon, its mixture of good and evil. And their history is a continuous witness to their corruption. Therefore, Paul's warning against being conformed is also valid for the Church. But is it possible, one may ask, to escape conformity if one belongs to a group that is united by a common creed, by rituals, by ethical standards, by old traditions and regular acts of common devotion? Can you adhere to a church and *not* be conformed? Indeed, there were non-conformist churches. But were they not non-conformist for only one historic moment, and then conformist themselves, like those from whom they separated? These are serious questions, especially for Protestants whose church came into existence through a protest against the conformity of the ruling church. I do not hesitate to state that one may have to resist being conformed even in the church community. Certainly, such an act also involves a risk. One may be in error. But it must be done. For it may represent the divine protest against everything human, even the highest forms of religion. A church in which this divine protest does not find a human voice through which it can speak has become conformed to this aeon. Here we see what non-conformity ultimately is – the resistance to idolatry, to making ultimates of ourselves and our world, our civilization and our church. And this resistance is the most difficult thing demanded of a man. It is so difficult that the prophets in the Old and New Testament, and the Reformers, and the leaders of the struggle against idolatry in the history of religion as a whole, when called to fight the conformity to this aeon, tried to escape this task. It is almost too difficult for human beings. It is not too difficult to become a critic and rebel. But it is hard not to be conformed to anything, not even to oneself, and to pronounce the divine judgment against idolatry, not so much because the courageous act may lead to suffering and martyrdom, but because of the risk of failure. It is hard because something in our conscience, a feeling of guilt, tries to prevent us from becoming non-conformist.

But even this feeling of guilt we must take upon ourselves. He who risks and fails can be forgiven. He who never risks and never fails is a failure in his whole being. He is not forgiven because he does not feel that he needs forgiveness. Therefore, dare to be not conformed to this aeon, but transform courageously first in yourselves, then in your world – in the spirit and the power of love.

13

Be Strong

Be watchful, stand firm in your faith, be courageous, be strong. Let all that you do be done in love.

I COR. 16.13–14

I

Out of this well-known passage, I chose two words on which I want you to centre your attention in this hour – be strong! They are surrounded in our text by other qualities that make strength possible – watchfulness, faith, courage, love. All together, they describe the strong Christian personality.

How can we attain strength? This is a question asked in all ages of man's life and in all periods of human history. It is a question asked with passion and despair in our time, and most impatiently by those who are no longer children and not yet adults.

In our text Paul uses the word 'be' several times: '*be* strong', he says to the Corinthians. We easily slip over it. But it should arrest our attention as fully as, and perhaps even more than, the main words of our text. For the word 'be' contains in its two letters the whole riddle of the relation of man to God.

Paul does not ask of the Christians in Corinth something that is strange to them. He asks them to be what they are, Christian personalities. All the imperatives he uses are descriptions of something that is, before they are demands for what ought to be. Be what you are – that is the only thing one can ask of any being. One cannot ask of a being to be something it was not before. It is as if life in all its forms desires to be asked, to receive demands. But no life can receive demands for something which it is not. It wants to be asked to become what it is and nothing else. This seems surprising, but a little thought shows us that it is true.

We know that one cannot ask fruits from thorns, or grain from weeds, or water from a dry fountain, or love from a cold heart, or courage from a cowardly mind, or strength from a weak life. If we ask such things from beings who do not have them, we are foolish; and either they will laugh at us or condemn us as unjust and hostile towards them. We can ask of anything or anyone only to bring forth what he has, to become what he is. Out of what is given to us, we can act. Receiving precedes acting.

'Be strong', says Paul. He says it to those who have received strength as he himself received strength when the power of a new reality grasped him. Now some of us will ask – 'what about us who feel that we have *not* received, and that we do not have faith and courage and strength and love? We are wanting in all these, so the commanding 'be' of Paul is not said to us. Or if it is said to us we remain unconcerned or become hostile towards him who says it. We are not strong, so nobody should ask us to be strong! We are weak. Shall we remain weak? Shall we fall into resignation, and become cynical about your demands? They may be for others. They are not for us.' I hear many people, more than we imagine, saying this. I hear whole classes of young people speaking thus. I hear many individuals in older generations repeating these words.

And I do not find any consolation in the Bible. There is the parable of the different soils on which the seed of the divine message falls and of which only *one* brings fruit. There is the word of the many who are called and *few* who are elected. There is the terrifying, realistic statement of Jesus that those to whom much is given will receive more, and that from those to whom little is given, even this will be taken away. There is the contrast between those who are born of light and have become its children and those who are born out of darkness and have become its children. There is the parable of the man as clay which cannot revolt against God the potter, no matter what the potter does to the clay. *We* would like to revolt, when we hear this. But if we look around us into the lives of men we are forced to say – 'So it is, the Bible is right!' We would like to say in good democratic phrasing – 'Everyone has a God-given chance to reach fulfilment, but not everybody uses it. Some do, some do not. Both have their ultimate destiny in their own hands.' We would like that to be so. But we cannot escape the truth that it *is not* so. The chances are *not* even. There is only a limited number of human beings to whom we can say – 'Be strong', because they are strong already. And the only honest thing I could say to the others, to whom many of us may belong, is – 'Accept that you are weak. Do not pretend that you are strong. And perhaps if you dare to be what you are, your weakness will become your strength. Accept that you are weak' – that is what we should say to those who *are* weak. 'Accept that you are a coward' – that is what we should say to those who are cowardly. 'Accept that you are wavering in the faith' – that is what we should say to those who are not firm in it. And to those who do not love, we should say – 'Accept that you are not able to love'.

This sounds strange! But everyone who knows the human soul, and knows his own soul above all, will understand what is meant. He will understand that the first step in becoming strong is to acknowledge and accept his weakness. He who does so will cease to deceive himself by saying to himself – 'I have at least something of what the apostle demands. He can demand it from me, for somehow I have it.' There are people who could rightly speak so to themselves. Yet there are others for whom such a judgment would be a self-deception. To them we must say – 'Accept that you are weak; be honest towards yourselves.'

Let me say to those who are responsible for others, as parents, teachers, ministers, counsellors, friends: do not say the demanding 'be' to anybody without fear and hesitation. If you use it, you approach the mystery of the divine election and you may destroy a life by demanding something of a person that he is not!

II

All these insights lie behind the first thing Paul asks of the Christians – namely, that they be watchful. The strong being is strong only if he watches his strength, aware of the fact that there is weakness in his strength. There is a non-Christian in every Christian. There is a weak being in every strong one. There is cowardice in every courage, and unbelief in every faith, and hostility in every love. Watchfulness means that the Christian never can rest on his being a Christian, that he who is strong can never rely on his strength.

One can be strong by subjecting oneself to a strong discipline. By suppressing much in oneself one may become powerful in relation to others. It is often this type that is called a strong personality. And, certainly, strength without the ability to direct oneself is not strength. But those who have this ability and are admired as strong personalities should be watchful: they should watch whether their strength has weakness at its basis, whether it excludes elements of life that constitute the richness and the glory of life. If they do not watch their hidden weakness, it may flow forth as hatred for those who affirm the abundance of life. This abundance they cannot endure, because it reveals the weakness on which their strength is built. In order to reassure themselves, they force upon others the same restrictions they have imposed on their own life. Their domineering strength creates weakness in others. There is a profound ambiguity about the strong Christian personality: Christianity could not live, society could not go on, without them. But many other Christians, many persons, who perhaps could have become strong themselves, are destroyed or reduced to mental weakness and often illness by them. They are the bearers of Christianity and society; but their victims among Christians and non-Christians, beginning with their children, their wives or their husbands, are numerous. Be watchful when you are considered, or consider yourselves, strong. Be watchful, and do not demand of those around you to be what you are, and what they are not. You will destroy them by your strength.

Those who are considered strong usually have a strong conviction. They seem to do what Paul asks them to – namely, to 'stand in the faith'. Everybody needs a place to stand upon. Without a foundation no strength is possible. In the physical universe it is a place on the well-grounded earth, as the Greeks said; no experience seems more disturbing, even for the strongest minds, than the shaking of the ground in an earthquake. In the social universe it is the home – the home town and the home country on which we stand; and from earliest times those who lost their homeland were considered weakest and most unprotected. What about the spiritual universe? Language is the place we stand on in the spiritual universe. For out of the word by which we grasp our world and our own being all other spiritual creations grow: knowledge and the arts, social traditions and philosophical beliefs. The word gives man the strength to build a world above the given world. It makes him the ruler of nature, as in the paradise story: he becomes the ruler over other living beings by giving them names. He who is strong in the spiritual universe is strong in the power of the word. A profound insight into human strength and human weakness is expressed in the story of the tower of Babel. Mankind was strong as long as it was united in one language. Its strength impelled it to enter the heavenly sphere. But when God wanted to destroy man's self-elevation and reveal his weakness, he confused the *one* language so that people no longer understood each other. We are in a similar situation today. Our period is weak, because we can no longer speak to each other. Each one has his own language, and the word has lost its power. It has become shallow and confused. We have experienced earthquake and exile in the spiritual world.

Paul asks the Corinthians to stand on something that is deeper than the physical and social and spiritual universe, something that cannot be shaken, because all levels of the universe rest upon it, their divine ground. To stand on this ground is, in Paul's words, to stand in the faith. He, of course, thinks of the faith in the form in which he has brought it to the Corinthians. But in this faith, faith itself is present – namely, the standing on the ultimate ground below any shaking and changing ground. Breaking the way to this ground is the meaning of the appearance of the Christ. 'Stand firm in your faith' means – do not give up that faith that alone can make you ultimately strong, because it gives you the ultimate ground on which to stand. Standing firm in one's faith does not mean adhering to a set of beliefs; it does not require us to suppress doubts about Christian or other doctrines, but points to something which lies beyond doubt in the depth in which man's being and all being is rooted. To be aware of this ground, to live in it and out of it is ultimate strength. 'Be strong' and 'stand in the faith' are one and the same command. But remembering now the word 'be', some may reply – 'Then the demand to be strong is not for us, because we do not stand in any faith. Doubt or unbelief is our destiny, not faith. We know you are right, there is no strength where there is no faith. But we have neither. And if there is some strength in us, it is the strength of honesty, the unwillingness to submit to a faith that is not ours, either for conventional reasons, or because of our longing for strength, or because of being taken in by our contemporary emotion-arousing evangelists. Our strength is to resist and to reject strength that is born of dishonesty.' Some of the best minds of our time would speak thus. To them I answer – 'Your honesty proves your faith and therefore your honesty is your strength! You may not believe in anything that can be stated in doctrines or symbols. But you stand on the ultimate ground, you stand firm in your faith as long as you stand in honesty and take your doubt and your unbelief seriously without restriction. Become aware of the faith that you *have*, and you will find words for it, perhaps even Christian words. But with or without words, be strong; for you *are* strong.'

Strength, according to Paul's words, includes courage. For human strength is built on human anxiety. Insecurity takes many forms. One of the most dangerous is the experience of being split within ourselves. He who is united with himself is invincibly strong. But who is? We are all dominated by forces that conquer parts of our being and split our personality. We have not merely lost the power of the word; we also have lost the strength that is given with a united, centred personality. We are disrupted by compulsions, known formerly as demonic powers. And who can command a split personality – 'Be strong!' To which side of the personality can such a command be addressed? Yet, there is the possibility of something else. Healing power, coming ultimately from the ground on which we stand in the faith, can enter the personality and unite it in an act of courage. It is the courage that takes upon itself the anxiety of our disruptions. This courage is the innermost centre of faith. It dares to affirm our being, while simultaneously rejecting it. Out of this courage the greatest strength emerges. It is the strength that overcomes the powers splitting world and soul. Be courageous! Say Yes to yourselves in spite of the anxiety of the No.

So Paul finishes his description of the strong personality: a courageous, watchful hero, firm in faith, worthy of great praise. But that is just what Paul does not do. Instead, he says – 'Let all that you do be done in love.' The strength of the personality whom Paul has in mind is based on something beyond courage and faith and watchfulness. It is not the strength of a hero. It is the strength of him who surrenders the praise he could receive as a hero to the humility of love. We are all familiar with strong personalities, perhaps in our families, among friends, or in public life, whom we admire, but in whom we feel something is wanting. This something is love. They may be friendly and be willing to help. This they demand of themselves. But everything they demand of themselves they also demand of others. They use the word 'be' without hesitation. They become tyrants through personal strength. Without love he who is strong becomes a law for the weak. And the law makes those who are weak even weaker. It drives them into despair, or rebellion, or indifference. Strength without love destroys, first others, then itself. For love is not something that may or may not be added to strength in its fullest sense; it is an element of strength. One cannot be strong without love. For love is not an irrelevant emotion; it is the blood of life, the power of reunion of the separated. Strength without love leads to separation, to judgment, to control of the weak. Love reunites what is separated; it accepts what is judged; it participates in what is weak, as God participates in our weakness and gives us strength by his participation.

14

In Thinking be Mature

Brethren, do not be children in your thinking; be babes in evil, but in thinking be mature.

I COR. 14.20

In thinking be mature! Such an admonition one would hardly expect in the context of apostolic writing. But here it is, appearing in the same letter of Paul in which he contrasts sharply the wisdom of the world with that foolishness of God that is wiser than the wisdom of men. And he points to the fact that not many wise men belong to the ranks of the congregation, but that God has chosen what is foolish in the world. Maturity on the basis of divine foolishness – this is hard to understand – not only for the first readers of the letter to the Corinthians, but for all generations of Christians and non-Christians in the history of Christianity. In some way, the whole problem of the possibility of Christian existence is implied in this combination of divine foolishness and human maturity. But perhaps it is not only the problem of the possibility of human existence as such – how to unite divine foolishness with human maturity. Certainly, it is as valid for everyone outside the Church as for those inside, when Paul says – 'Whoever of you imagines that he is wise with this world's wisdom must become a fool if he is really to be wise' (3.18).

It is not this foolishness that conflicts with maturity, but the state of spiritual infancy, the state of being a babe in thinking, unable to receive solid food, milk-fed only. Paul complains that even now the Corinthians are not ready for solid food, that they are still immature, as shown in their theological jealousies and quarrels, that they are still far away from the divine foolishness, which is what makes them immature.

What does it mean to be mature in thinking? We speak of maturity in scholarly education, tested by examinations and scientific work. In some countries the basic examination for higher education is called 'examination of maturity'. But are those who have passed and become students in a professional school really mature in thinking? Are their teachers mature in thinking? Is the great scholar mature in thinking? If maturity means having mastered one's professional field and being able to work creatively in it, the great scholar, the good teacher, and his best pupils, are mature. And most of us, then, who are gathered here today should be able to call ourselves mature. We should not need the admonition – be mature in thinking!

But we do need it, both those who live within the Christian tradition and those who are outside it. We are *not* mature in thinking, not even those among us who are called outstanding scholars within and beyond the Christian horizon. Our immaturity is our lack of divine foolishness.

It might be well first to consider those who feel at home within the churches. It seems that faithful and active members often feel more certain of their own maturity than do those who stand aside in criticism and doubt. But their belief witnesses to their immaturity. This sense of certainty is understandable, however, when one realizes that it stems from an institution that has matured through centuries in life and thought, and whose foundation is the picture of the most mature personal life, that of Jesus as the Christ, in whom, at the same time, divine foolishness is manifest in every moment. Belonging to this community gives the members a feeling of being mature themselves. But they are not and, as Protestants, we must add that not even their churches are. For who is mature?

A mature man is one who has reached his natural power in life and thought and is able to use it freely. Maturity in thinking does not mean reaching the end of one's thinking, but rather the state in which the human power of thought is at one's disposal. This is the state we are asked to attain, but this is where we always fall short – first, the Christians, and then those who question Christianity. The Christian churches and individuals often vary their power of thinking, because they believe that radical thought conflicts with the divine foolishness that underlies all wisdom. But this is not true, certainly not for biblical thinking. Radical thought conflicts with human foolishness, with spiritual infancy, with ignorance, superstition and intellectual dishonesty. It is the temptation of the churches in all generations to justify their human foolishness by calling it divine foolishness. This is their defence against becoming mature in thinking. But although Christianity is based on the message of the divine foolishness, it knows that, out of the acceptance of this message, mature thinking can grow courageously and abundantly. What prevents it from growing is that the guardians of the message, churches and individual Christians, imprison the divine foolishness in vessels and forms that are produced by a wisdom that is mixed with foolishness, as is all human wisdom. And if these forms and vessels are declared indestructible and unchangeable, the way to maturity in thinking is barred. For the decisive step to maturity is risking the break away from spiritual infancy with its protective traditions and guiding authorities. Without 'no' to authority, there is no maturity. This 'no' need not be rebellious, arrogant, or destructive. As long as it is so, it indicates immaturity by this very attitude.

The 'no' that leads to maturity can be, and basically always is, experienced in anxiety, in discouragement, in guilt feelings, and despairing inner struggles. For the infant spiritual state with its traditions and authorities is invested with the holiness of man's ultimate concern and gives spiritual security and primitive strength. It is hard to break away from it. And, certainly, the way to maturity in thinking is a difficult path. Much must be left behind: early dreams, poetic imaginations, cherished legends, favoured doctrines, accustomed laws and ritual traditions. Some of them must be restored on a deeper level, some must be given up. Despite this price, maturity can be gained – a manly, self-critical, convincing faith, not *produced* by reasoning, but *reasonable*, and at the same time rooted in the message of the divine foolishness, the ultimate source of wisdom. A Church that is able to show this way to its members, and to follow the path itself, has certainly reached maturity.

And now I want to turn to those who consider themselves to be outside the Church and feel indifferent towards it, or perhaps even critical, hostile or fanatical in their negation. For them, too, the word of the apostle is as valid as it is for the Church – be mature in thinking! It is not difficult, nor worthwhile, to deal with the petty immaturities of the secular mind. It is challenging and worthwhile, however, to penetrate to the source of its basic immaturity and to apply Paul's admonition to those who believe that they are mature just *because* they consider themselves to be outside the Church. No representative of the Church should criticize them carelessly, as if speaking with the possession of maturity to those who are immature. Nor should a church representative criticize the secular world before having subjected the Church to the same serious scrutiny. And if he cannot do this in both directions with love, he should refrain from doing it altogether.

It is for this reason that I prefer not to refute the attacks of the secular mind on the Church. The self-criticism of the Church, as shown before, goes deeper than could any such attack. Also, I do not want to criticize any of the creative activities of the secular mind, the sciences, the arts, social relations, technical activities, and politics. These disciplines have their own criteria and their leaders apply these criteria with severity, honesty and self-criticism. In all this the secular mind is mature and religion should never interfere with it, as mature science would never interfere with religious symbols, since they lie in another dimension of experience and reality. To discuss the existence or non-existence of God as a being alongside other beings betrays the utter immaturity on both sides. It betrays complete ignorance about the meaning and power of the divine.

The secular mind, however, encounters a basic impediment to reaching maturity in thinking. It turns away from the divine foolishness found in the ground of its wisdom, and this makes its wisdom, however successful in conquering the world, humanly foolish. 'Be mature in thinking' is said to the great scholar as urgently as to the ordinary member of a congregation. For possessing a perfect brain does not ensure maturity, nor does having a creative mind mean that one is mature. There is no maturity where the awareness of the divine foolishness is lacking. So then, what is meant by this apparent paradox?

It is born out of an experience that cuts through all other experiences, shaking them, turning them to a new direction, and raising them beyond themselves. It is the experience of something ultimate, inexhaustible in meaning, unapproachable in being, unconquerable in power. We may call it the holy, the eternal, the divine. It is beyond every name because it is present in everything that has a name, in you and in me. If we try to utter it, we speak of the unspeakable; yet we *must* speak of it. For it is nearer to us than our own self, and yet it is more removed from us than the farthest galaxies. Such experience is the most human of all experiences. One can cover it up, one can repress it, but never totally. It is effective in the restlessness of the heart, in the anxious question of one's own value, in the fear of losing the meaning of one's life, in the anxiety of emptiness, guilt, and of having to die. Myth, poetry, and the philosophy of mankind everywhere express this experience. They witness to things that are deeply buried in the human heart and in the depth of our world. But sometimes they break through the surface with eruptive power. No artist, philosopher, or scientist is mature who has never questioned himself and his experience as an artist, as a philosopher, or as a scientist. No mature scholar is humanly mature who has not asked the question of the meaning of his existence. A scholar who rightly takes nothing for granted in his scholarly work, but who takes his being as a scholar and his being as a man for granted is immature.

But if he is pressed hard by the question of his existence so that he cannot push it aside, he is ready to be grasped by divine foolishness. Even more, he is already grasped by it. He is driven out of the safe reasonableness of his daily life. He must face a depth in himself of which he was not aware before, a depth of dangers and promises, of darkness and expectations. And what he finds in himself he sees reflected in his world, a depth that was hidden to him before he found it in himself. Now he has become aware of it in others, in everything alive, in the whole universe. And if he receives answers to the questions awakened in him, he can listen to them, even if their grammar and their style sound ecstatic and paradoxical, measured by the language of daily life. Such answers, received, are what faith means. They sound like sacred foolishness, but are armed with the power of truth. If, however, they are brought to the level of ordinary reasonableness and attacked or defended on this level, they sound untrue, meaningless, absurd, whether accepted or rejected. The name of the language of divine foolishness and of the life that is created by it, is love. Love is life under the power of divine foolishness. It is ecstatic and paradoxical. It cuts through the ordinary ways of life, elevating them to a higher level. But if love is brought down to the level of moral reasonableness, and is attacked or defended on this basis, it becomes sentimental, utopian, and unreal.

The divine foolishness of thought and the divine foolishness of life are united in the symbol of Christmas: God *in* the infant, God *as* infant, anticipating and preparing the symbol of Good Friday – God *in* the condemned slave, God *as* the condemned slave. This certainly is ecstatic and paradoxical, and it should not be brought down to the level of a divine-human chemistry. But it should be understood and experienced as an expression of the divine foolishness that is the source of wisdom and the power of maturity. Be mature in thinking. Be mature in love!

15

On Wisdom

The fear of the Lord is the beginning of Wisdom. And the awareness of the Holy is insight.

PROV. 9.10

I

It was a grave loss when the term 'wisdom' almost disappeared from Christian preaching and teaching. Of course, it is still used sometimes in both popular and philosophical language. But its original significance and power have vanished. It has been called 'the virtue of old age', which is of no concern to youth. It has almost become as ridiculous as the ancient word 'virtue' itself.

One speaks of experience, insight, knowledge; and indeed those are related to wisdom and often part of it. But none of them is wisdom itself. Wisdom is greater than these. It is one of the great things that profoundly concern every human being in every period of his conscious life. Wisdom is not bound to old age. It is found equally in the young. And there are fools at all ages of life. It is my hope in this hour to communicate the meaning and the greatness of wisdom, particularly to those who are young and who must make wise decisions about their lives.

To understand the meaning of wisdom we must see it in the breadth and depth in which it was seen by the man whose words are our lesson. There are many more words about the glory of wisdom, both in the Old and the New Testament. And there is praise of wisdom and passionate seeking for it in many religions. Wisdom is universally human. It is present in the spiritual life of all mankind. And it is present not only in all mankind, but in the universe itself. For the universe is created by the divine power in the presence of Wisdom. This is the vision of the author of the book of Proverbs and of the poet who wrote the book of Job. Wisdom was beside God before creation of the world. 'When he marked out the foundations of the earth, then I was beside him', Wisdom says. 'When he gave to the wind its weight and meted out the waters by measure; when he made a decree for the rain and a way for the lightning of the thunder, he saw Wisdom then and studied her.' The meaning of these words is that God explores Wisdom, which is like an independent power beside him, and according to what he finds in her he forms the world. The universe in all its parts is the embodiment of wisdom.

This vision was confirmed for me a few weeks ago when I met some well-known astronomers, physicists and biologists, who passionately expressed their conviction that they increased the awareness of the eternal wisdom in the structure of the universe by increasing the knowledge of our world. They rejected a science that gives knowledge without wisdom and a theology that neglects the divine wisdom shining through man's knowledge of nature.

At the height of the Middle Ages in the thirteenth century, when methods of scientific research were first introduced, a keen observer made the prophetic remark: 'Under the new method science will increase but wisdom will decrease.' Wisdom was for him the understanding of the principles which determine life and world. He was right: science conquered wisdom; knowledge replaced insight. From century to century it has become more and more evident that knowledge without wisdom produces external and internal self-destruction.

The health of the younger generation is demonstrated by the fact that it has experienced and violently expressed the emptiness of knowledge without wisdom. Those who feel dissatisfied with learning facts without an understanding of their meaning, and those who feel the emptiness of the possession of knowledge without wisdom are most important in our academic and national society. May they never cease to express this feeling! May they force us, the older ones, to listen! But we shall *only* listen, if contempt of knowledge and scholarship does not colour their complaints; then we shall try

with all that is given to us to become their helpers on the road to
wisdom.

II

Wisdom is not easy to find. It remains a divine mystery in spite of
its presence in all parts of the universe. Wherever wisdom has been
praised in literature, its mystery has been recognized. The book
of Job asks – 'Where shall wisdom be and where is the place of
understanding? Man does not know the way to it and it is not found
in the land of the living. The deep says: Not in me and the sea
says: not in me. It is hidden from the eyes of all living and concealed
from the birds of the air; only abyss and death say: we have heard
a rumour of it with our ears.' This means that wisdom is not a
human possibility. The praise of wisdom is not a praise of man and
his power. Only abyss and death – the boundary line of human
existence – point to wisdom, but even they cannot give it. They
have heard about it only from a distance, the poet says. Wisdom is
not a matter of intellectual power; rationality is not wisdom. Death
says more about wisdom than life; but death does not have the
answer.

Why is wisdom so hidden, although manifest in everything that
is? It is because in everything that lives there are two forces at battle
with each other – a creative force and a destructive one, both of
which emanate from the same divine ground. As the book of Job
says – 'With God is wisdom and might; he has counsel and understanding. If *he* tears down, none can rebuild, if *he* shuts a man in,
none can open. Power and providence belong to him, he is behind
deceiver and deceived; he strips statesmen of their wits and makes
a fool of councillors. . . . he will extend a nation to destroy it, he
will enlarge a nation to enslave it . . . Should not his majesty cause
you to shudder?' No one can doubt that this is the way life is, but
our poet knows that behind all this is the mystery of divine wisdom.
Wisdom is in both creation and destruction. This is the deepest
insight the Old Testament reached. Without it the men of the New
Testament would not have been able to endure the cross of him

whom they called the Christ. Without it Paul could not have broken
into the words – 'O the depth of the riches and wisdom and knowledge of God', just after he had spoken with an aching heart of the
rejection of his nation for the sake of the Gentiles. Wisdom and
mystery do not exclude each other. It is wisdom to see wisdom in
the mystery and the conflicts of life.

III

But now we ask – how can we possess such wisdom? In the book
of Proverbs, Wisdom says – 'I was . . . rejoicing before him always,
rejoicing in his inhabited world and delighting in the sons of men
. . . and now, my sons, listen to me . . . he who finds me, finds life
. . . but all who hate me love death.' To aspire to wisdom, or to
despise it, is a matter of life and death. This could never be said of
knowledge in the ordinary sense of the word. Those who know
much do not have life because of their knowledge. And those who
know little, and do not try to learn much, do not prove that they
love death. Wisdom is a matter of life and death because it is more
than knowledge. It can be united with knowledge, but it can also
stand alone. It belongs to a dimension which cannot be reached by
scholarly endeavour. It is insight into the meaning of one's life, into
its conflicts and dangers, into its creative and destructive powers,
and into the ground out of which it comes and to which it must
return.

Therefore, the preachers of wisdom tell us that the first step in
acquiring it is the fear of God and the awareness of the holy. Such
words can easily be misunderstood. They do not command subjection to a god who arouses fear. Nor do they advise us to accept
doctrines about him. Such a command and such advice would lead
us straight away from wisdom and not towards it. But our text says
that there cannot be wisdom without an encounter with the holy,
with that which creates awe, and shakes the ordinary way of life
and thought. Without the experience of awe in face of the mystery
of life, there is no wisdom. Most removed from wisdom are not
those who are driven by desire for pleasure or power, but those

brilliant minds who have never encountered the holy, who are without awe and know nothing sacred, but who are able to conceal their ultimate emptiness by the brilliant performances of their intellect. No wisdom shines through the knowledge of many men who play a great role in our academic and non-academic society. The wisdom at which God looks in the creation of the world, the eternal wisdom, calls them fools.

He who has encountered the mystery of life has reached the source of wisdom. In encountering it with awe and longing, he experiences the infinite distance of his being from that which is the ground of his being. He experiences the limits of his being, his finitude in face of the infinite. He learns that acceptance of one's limits is the decisive step towards wisdom. The fool rebels against the limits set by his finitude. He wants to be unlimited in power and knowledge. He who is wise accepts his finitude. He knows that he is not God.

To this all mankind's literature about wisdom is a witness. Wisdom is the acknowledgment of limits; it is the awareness of the right measure in all relations of life. But in saying this, one must protect wisdom against a dangerous distortion of its meaning – the confusion of wisdom with a philistine avoidance of radical decisions, with clever compromises and shrewd calculations of usefulness, all of which is far removed from the wisdom that comes upon us in the awe-inspiring encounter with the holy. We need only look at the great figures in whom men of all periods and cultures recognized wisdom, the men who gave new laws to their nations, the teachers of new ways of life for continents, the men who withdrew to the deserts of nature and the deserts of the soul to return with abundance. None of them kept to the middle of the road; they had to find new roads in the wilderness. You cannot find wisdom in those who always avoid radical decisions and adjust themselves to the given situation, the conformists who have decided to accept the accepted opinions of society. Wisdom loves the children of men, but she prefers those who come through foolishness to wisdom, and dislikes those who keep themselves equally distant from foolishness and from wisdom. They are the real fools, she would say, because they were never shaken by an encounter with the mystery of life, and therefore never able to see the unity of creation and destruction in the working of the divine wisdom. In those, however, who have recognized this working of wisdom, and become wise by it, artificial limits are broken down, often with great pain, and the real limits, the true measures, are found. That is what happens when wisdom comes to men.

Therefore, wisdom comes to all men, and not only to those who are learned. You can find quiet and often great wisdom among very simple people. There may be wise ones among those with whom you live, and those with whom you work, and those whom you encounter as strangers in crowded streets. There is wisdom in mothers and lonely women, in children and adolescents, in shepherds and cab-drivers; and sometimes there is wisdom also in those who have much learning. They all prove their wisdom by creatively accepting their limits and their finitude.

But who can accept his finitude? Who can accept that he is threatened by the vicissitudes of life, by sickness, by death? Who can take into himself the deep anxiety of being alive without covering it up with pleasure and activity? In the book of Job, which powerfully expresses the mystery of life, the question is asked and an answer given that is not an answer in the ordinary sense of the word. Only in the confrontation with eternal wisdom in all its darkness and inexhaustible depth can man accept the misery of his finitude, even if it is as extreme as Job's. In our encounter with the holy, facing with awe the ultimate mystery of life, we experience a dimension of life that gives us the courage and the strength to accept our limits and to become wise through this acceptance.

IV

In the literature about wisdom many special rules for our daily life are given. The Bible is full of them. But they are all connected with each other in that they all are ruled by the encounter with the holy. In all of them wisdom appears as the acceptance of one's finitude. In the light of this insight, let us look at expressions of wisdom in our daily life. Wisdom is present in parents who know the limits of their authority and so do not become idols first and crushed idols later. Wisdom is present in children who recognize the limits of their independence and do not despise the heritage they have received and on which they live, even in rebelling against their parents. Wisdom is present in teachers who are aware of their limits in dealing both with truth and with their pupils, and who ask themselves again and again whether wisdom shines through the knowledge they communicate. Wisdom is present in students who question the principles behind whatever they are studying and its meaning for their lives; wise are they who realize both the necessity and the limits of all learning and the superiority of love over knowledge. Wise are those men who are aware of their emotional and intellectual limitations as men in their encounter with women. Wise are those women who acknowledge their finitude by accepting the man as the other pole of a common humanity. And both show wisdom if they accept each other without anxiety, without hostility, without abuse, without dishonesty, but in the power of a love which is rooted in the awareness of the eternal.

The greatest wisdom is needed where it is most painful to accept our finitude – in our failures, errors, and the guilt acquired by our foolishness. It is hard for us to accept failure, perhaps total failure, in our work. It is difficult to acknowledge error, perhaps in our judgment of those we love in friendship or marriage. It is humanly impossible to confess guilt to oneself or to others without looking at that which is greater than our heart, the eternal. He who possesses this wisdom, this painfully acquired wisdom, knows that nothing can separate him from the eternal wisdom which is with God, neither failure nor error nor guilt.

Our final wisdom is to accept our foolishness and to look at the place in history in which wisdom itself appeared in the garb of utter foolishness, the Cross of the Christ. Here the wisdom that is eternally with God, that is present in the universe, and that loves the children of man, appears in fullness. And in those who look at it and receive it, faith and wisdom become one.

16

In Everything Give Thanks

Rejoice always, pray without ceasing, in everything give thanks.
I THESS. 5.16–18

I

'In everything give thanks.' These are the words that we want to make the centre of our meditation. Do we need this admonition? Is not 'thank you' one of the most frequently employed phrases in our language? We use it constantly for the smallest services performed, for a friendly word, for every word praising ourselves and our acts. We use it whether we are grateful or not. Saying thanks has become a form that is employed with or without feeling. We must therefore say it with great emphasis and in strong words when we really mean it. Anyone who observes the behaviour of religious groups – ministers as well as laymen – is familiar with their inclination to say 'thank you' to God almost as often as to their neighbours. It seems important, therefore, to ask the reason for this behaviour towards men and God. Why do we thank? What does it mean to give thanks and to receive thanks? Can this event of our daily life, and of daily religious life, be understood in its depth and elevated above automatic superficiality? If this proves possible, we might discover that the simple 'thank you' can tell us much about what we are within ourselves and our world. We might find that one of the most used and abused words of our language can become a revelation of the deeper levels of our being.

Saying thanks is not always merely a form of social intercourse. Often we are driven by real emotion; we are almost compelled to thank someone, whether he expects it or not. And sometimes our emotion overpowers us and we say thanks in words much too strong for the gift we have received. This is not dishonest. It is honestly felt in the moment. But soon afterwards we feel somehow empty, somehow ashamed – not much perhaps, but a little! Occasionally, it also happens that for one moment we feel abundantly grateful. But since, for external reasons, we have no immediate opportunity to express our thanks, we forget it and it never reaches the one to whom we are grateful. Of the ten lepers who were healed by Jesus probably none was without abundant gratefulness to Jesus, but only one returned from the priests to whom they had shown themselves to thank Jesus. And Jesus was astonished and disappointed.

Not only are we driven by a deep emotion to give thanks, but we also have a profound need to receive thanks when we have given ourselves in either a large or small way. When thanks is not forthcoming, we feel a kind of emptiness, a vacuum in that place of our inner being which the words or acts of thanks should fill. But just as we feel ashamed when we use too strong an expression of gratitude, we feel uneasy when we receive exaggerated thanks. There is no place in us to receive it and we refuse to accept it, whether we say so or not. It is always difficult to receive thanks without some resistance. The American reply, 'you are welcome', or the German reply, 'please', expresses the refusal to accept thanks without hesitation. 'Don't mention it' is the simplest expression of this resistance to accept thanks, which, however, we *do* accept at the same time.

These uncertainties in the simple act of giving or receiving thanks teach us something about our relationship to others, and our predicament. In every act of giving or receiving thanks, we accept or reject someone, and we are accepted or rejected by someone. Such acceptance or rejection is not always noticed, either by ourselves or by the other. If we are sensitive, we often feel it and react with joy or sorrow, with shame or pride, and mostly with mixtures of these emotions. A simple 'thank you' can be an attack or a withdrawal. It can be the expression of giving someone a place within us, or a successful way of protecting ourselves from someone's attempt to find a place within us. A word of thanks can be a complete rejection of him whom we thank, or it can be the unlocking of his and our heart. But probably in most cases, it is a polite form of stating that he whom we thank does not really concern us very much.

The fiftieth Psalm says – 'Offer to God a sacrifice of thanksgiving', and 'He who brings thanksgiving as his sacrifice honours me'. Here the original meaning of thanks shines through. Giving thanks is a sacrifice. Here the literal meaning of 'thanksgiving' is felt. Thanks is expressed through sacrificial acts. Valuable objects are removed from their ordinary use and given to the gods. It is an acknowledgment of the fact that man did not create himself, that nothing belongs to him, that naked he was thrown into the world and naked he will be thrust out of it. What he has is given to him. In the act of sacrifice he expresses his awareness of this destiny. He gives a part of what is given to him, but something that is ultimately not his own. In sacrificing thanks he witnesses to his finitude, to his transitoriness. Every serious giving of thanks implies a sacrifice, an acknowledgment of one's finitude. A man who is able to thank seriously accepts that he is creature and, in acceptance, he is religious even though he denies religion. And a man who is able to accept honest thanks without embarrassment is mature. He knows his own finitude as well as that of the other, and he knows that the mutual sacrifice of thanks confirms that he and the other are creatures.

II

In all expressions of gratitude towards others, the object of our thanks is usually visible. We know at least *whom* to thank, and what for, although we often do not know *how* to thank. But there is also gratefulness that is, so to speak, without a definite object towards which to turn. This is so not because we do not know the object, but because there is no object. We are simply grateful. Thankfulness has taken hold of us, not because something special has happened to us, but just because we *are*, because we participate in the glory and power of being. It is a mood of joy, but more than a mood, more than a transitory emotion. It is a state of being. And it is more than joy. It is a joy that includes the feeling that it is given, that we cannot accept it without bringing some sacrifice – namely, the sacrifice of thanks. But there is no one to whom we can bring it. And so it remains within us, a state of silent gratefulness.

You may ask – why is not God the object of such gratefulness? But that would not describe what happens in many men – Christians as well as non-Christians, believers and unbelievers. They are grateful. But they do not turn to God with direct words of prayer. It is just gratefulness in itself which fills them. If they were told to turn to *God* in a prayer of thanks, they would feel that such a command would destroy their spontaneous experience of gratefulness. How shall we judge this state of mind that many of us may have experienced at some time? Shall we say it is thanks without God, and therefore not real thanks? Shall we say that in this state we are like the pagans of whom Paul says that 'although they knew God, they did not honour him as God or give thanks to him'? Certainly not. The abundance of a grateful heart gives honour to God even if it does not turn to him in words. An unbeliever who is filled with thanks for his very being has ceased to be an unbeliever. His rejoicing is a spontaneous obedience to the exhortation of our text – 'Rejoice always!'

It is then possible to understand our text when it says – 'Rejoice *always*, pray *without ceasing*, give thanks in everything!' It certainly does not mean – 'never feel sorrow, day and night use words of prayer and thanks!' Jesus characterizes this way of imposing oneself on God as a perversion of religion. Then what do these exhortations mean? They mean just what we called the state of silent gratefulness, that may or may not express itself in prayers. We are not to tell God without ceasing what we wish him to do for us or what he has done for us. We are asked to rise to God always and in all things. He shall never be absent from our awareness. Certainly, he is creatively present in everyone in every moment whether we are aware of it or not. But when we are in the state of silent gratefulness, we *are* aware of his presence. We experience an elevation of life that we cannot attain by profuse words of thanks, but that can happen to us if we are open to it. A man was once asked if he prayed. He answered, 'always and never'. He meant that he was aware of the divine presence, but only rarely did he use words of prayer and thanks to express this awareness. He did not belong to those who do not thank because they are never aware of the presence of the divine, and he did not belong to those who believe that being aware of God means addressing him continuously. He thought that words directed towards God must come out of a state of elevation, of silent gratefulness. Another man was asked whether he believed in God, and he answered, 'I don't know, but if something very good happens to me, I need someone to whom I can give thanks.' He experienced the state of grateful elevation, like the first, but he was driven to express his feelings in direct words of thanks. He had need of another to whom to sacrifice. Both men describe the fact that thanking God is a state of elevation without words and also a desire to sacrifice in words directed to God.

In these two ways of thanking, two kinds of relationship to God are manifest: He is the other to whom I speak in words of thanks: and he is above myself and every other, the one to whom I cannot speak, but who can make himself manifest to me through a state of silent gratefulness.

One of the great and liberating experiences of the Protestant reformers was their realization that our relation to God is not dependent on the continuous repetition of words of prayer and thanks directed to God, on sacrifices and other rituals but rather on the serenity and joy that is the answer to the good news that we are accepted by God because of his seeking us, and not because of anything we can do or say in and outside the church.

III

For what do we give thanks? Are there limits to giving thanks? Our text says – 'In *everything* give thanks!' This does not mean – give thanks for everything, but give thanks in every situation! There are no limits to situations in which to thank, but there are limits to things for which thanks can be expressed. This is again a question the answer to which might lead us into a new understanding of the human predicament.

In the letter to I Tim. 4.4 we read – 'For everything created by

God is good and nothing is to be rejected if it is received with thanksgiving; for then it is consecrated by the word of God and prayer.' In these words, thanksgiving receives a new function. It consecrates everything created by God. Thanksgiving is consecration; it transfers something that belongs to the secular world into the sphere of the holy. It is not transformed, as superstition in and outside of Christian beliefs would transform it, but it is elevated to represent the divine. It has become a bearer of grace. Therefore, we say 'grace' when we give thanks for our daily food, and thus consecrate it. Every created thing can be a bearer of holiness, an object of thanks, of consecration. There are no limits to thanksgiving in this respect. We can give thanks for our bodily and our mental powers, for the darkness of our unconscious as well as for the light of our consciousness, for the abundance of nature and the creations of history, for everything that is and manifests its power of being. We can give thanks for all these despite their rejection by those who, through world-hating asceticism and fanatical puritanism, blaspheme the God of creation. Everything for which we can give thanks with a good conscience is consecrated by our thanks. This is not merely a profound theological insight; it is also a practical standard in situations where we are uncertain about accepting or rejecting something. If, after having accepted it, we can give thanks for it, we witness to its goodness as created. In giving thanks seriously, we consecrate it to the holy source of being from which it comes. And we even take the risk that Protestant Christians must take – that their conscience may fall into error and consecrate something which should be rejected.

There are no limits to giving thanks in the whole of creation. But are there not limits in our life? Can we honestly give thanks for the frustrations, accidents, and diseases that strike us? We *cannot* in the moment when they take hold of us. Here is one of the many situations where piety can degenerate into dishonesty. For we rightly resist such evils. We want to remove them; we are often angry against our destiny and its divine ground. And there are depths of suffering, bodily and mental, in which even the question of thanking or not thanking does not appear. Out of the depths the psalmist *cries* to God; he does *not* thank him. This is honest, realistic – a realism born out of the awareness of the divine presence. And I believe that at some time in our lives all of us have had experiences that were nothing but evil when they happened, but that became good later and the object of honest thanks.

And we also cannot give thanks for our own acts that make us guilty or for those that make us good. We cannot give thanks for that which makes us guilty; and sometimes things for which we have given thanks become evil by our own guilt. Nor should we give thanks for that in us which makes us good. The thanks of the Pharisee for his good works is an outstanding example of thanks which should *not* be given. In reality, he does not thank *God* when he is thankful for his own goodness, but thanks himself. How many of us thank ourselves when we give thanks to God! But one *cannot* thank oneself, because the sacrifice of thanking, if given to oneself, ceases to be a sacrifice. Thanks to oneself is not thanks, even when prayers of thanks to God are hidden ways of thanking oneself, as after work well done or success achieved by great toil.

It is a surprising experience to read the Bible, and especially the last third of the book of Psalms, with the question of thanks in one's mind. One discovers that the praise of God fills page after page in which the misery of all men, including the writers of these books, is also most drastically described. Reading them, we feel as though we walk in another realm. We cannot reproduce in ourselves what is happening to these men. (*We* are not in the mood of praising, hardly in the mood of thanking.) We look into the depth of our predicament and do not see much reason for praise and thanks. And if we think that it is our duty to God to thank him, or if we participate in church services that include praise and thanks, we do not feel that we have truly expressed our state of mind. Although this experience is not invariable, it is a predominant trait of our religious situation. It expresses itself in the messages of the best of our present preachers and theologians. It is a dominating theme of our great poets and philosophers. We are not called to pass judgment on these men. We have a part in them. They express *us* as they express themselves. And we should thank those who do it seriously, and often out of deep spiritual suffering.

The difference between our situation and that of former periods becomes visible when we read about the passion and intensity with which the members of the early Church gave thanks for the gift of the Christian message in a world of pagan glory, disintegration and despair. Is the same passion and intensity in us when we give thanks for the gift of God which is the Christ and his Church? Who can honestly answer 'yes'?

And do we not sense the same differences when we read how the fighters of the Reformation thanked God for the rediscovery of the good news of the divine acceptance of those who are sinners? Is the same infinite concern in us as was in them? Who can honestly answer 'yes'? We must therefore be grateful to those who express our present situation honestly.

But there is one consolation: we are not separated from the ever active presence of God, and we can become aware of it in every moment. Our hearts can become filled with praise and thanks without the use of words; and sometimes we may also find these words of praise and thanks. But this is not the first step, and often not even the last. Let us not follow those who use what is called 'the present religious revival' to force us back into forms of prayer and thanks that we cannot honestly accept, or that produce joy and thanks through self-suggestion. But let us keep ourselves open to the power that carries our life in every moment, that is here and now, that comes to us through nature and through the message of Jesus as the Christ. May we keep open to it, so that we may be filled with silent gratefulness for the power of being which is in us. And then perhaps words of thanks, words of sacrifice and consecration, may come to our tongues, so that we again may give thanks in truth and honesty.

PRAYER

Almighty God! We raise our hearts to thee in praise and thanks. For we are not by ourselves and nothing is ours except what thou hast given us. We are finite; we did not bring anything into our world; we shall not take anything out of our world. Thou hast given us the life which is ours so long as it is thy will. We thank thee that we have being, that we share in the inexhaustible riches of life, in the smallest and in the largest part of it. We praise thee when we feel strength in body and soul. We give thanks to thee when joy fills our hearts. We are gratefully aware of thy presence, be it in silence, or in words.

Awaken us to such awareness when our daily life hides thy presence from us, when we forget how near thou art to us in every place and in every moment, nearer than any other being is to us, nearer than we are to ourselves. Let us not turn away from thy giving and creating presence to the things thou hast given us. Let us not forget the creator behind the creation. Keep us always ready for the sacrifice of giving thanks to thee.

Thine is what we are and have. We consecrate it to thee. Receive our thanks when we say grace, consecrating our food and with it all that we receive in our daily life. Prevent us from using empty words and forms when we give thanks to thee. Save us from routine and mere convention when we dare to speak to thee.

We thank thee when we look back at our life, be it long or short, for all that we have met in it. And we thank thee not only for what we have loved and for what gave us pleasure, but also for what brought us disappointment, pain and suffering, because we *now* know that it helped to us to fulfil that for which we were born. And if new disappointments and new suffering takes hold of us and words of thanks die on our tongues, remind us that a day may come when we will be ready to give thanks for the dark road on which thou hast led us.

Our words of thanks are poor and often we cannot find words at all. There are days and months and years in which we were or are still unable to speak to thee. Give us the power, at such times, to keep our hearts open to the abundance of life, and in silent gratefulness, to experience thy unchanging, eternal presence. Take the silent sacrifice of a heart when words of thanks become rare in us. Accept our silent gratefulness and keep our hearts and our minds open to thee always!

We thank thee for what thou hast given to this nation far beyond the gifts to any other nation! Let us remain thankful for it, so that we may overcome the dangers of shallowness of life and emptiness of heart that threaten our people. Prevent us from turning thy gifts into causes of injury and self-destruction. Let a grateful mind protect us against national and personal disintegration. Turn us to thee, the source of our being, eternal God! *Amen.*

A Word from the Preacher

Most of these sermons were delivered in university and college chapels, as were those in the preceding volumes, *The Shaking of the Foundations* and *The New Being*. The present collection dates from 1955 to 1963. The title 'The Eternal Now', taken from a sermon in the second section of the book, indicates that the presence of the Eternal in the midst of the temporal is a decisive emphasis in most of the sermons. I could have chosen 'The Spiritual Presence' as the general title, but the many unfavourable connotations with which the word 'spiritual' is burdened excluded this possibility. Only for a particular sermon in which every sentence interpreted the meaning of 'spiritual', could the word be used.

It is my hope that this collection, like its predecessors, will show that the Christian message – be it expressed in abstract theology or concrete preaching – is relevant for our time if it uses the language of our time.

My thanks go to Mrs Elisabeth Wood, who did the hard and necessary work of stylistic correction, as she has for the earlier volumes.

I dedicate this book to the memory of a man whose friendship has enriched and deepened the largest part of my adult life, and with whom I experienced moments in which the Spiritual Presence was manifest.

Chicago, May 1963   PAUL TILLICH

Lightning Source UK Ltd.
Milton Keynes UK
UKOW05f0315111013

218861UK00001B/6/P